1

This book belongs to:

_____

Taurus Daily Horoscope 2025

Author's Note: Time set to EDT and EST Zone (UTC-4, UTC-5)

Mystic Cat
Suite 41906, 3/2237 Gold Coast HWY
Mermaid Beach, Queensland, 4218
Australia
islandauthor@hotmail.com

Contents

The 12 Zodiac Star Signs

2026

January
S	M	T	W	T	F	S
				1	2	3
4	5	6	7	8	9	10
11	12	13	14	15	16	17
18	19	20	21	22	23	24
25	26	27	28	29	30	31

February
S	M	T	W	T	F	S
1	2	3	4	5	6	7
8	9	10	11	12	13	14
15	16	17	18	19	20	21
22	23	24	25	26	27	28

March
S	M	T	W	T	F	S
1	2	3	4	5	6	7
8	9	10	11	12	13	14
15	16	17	18	19	20	21
22	23	24	25	26	27	28
29	30	31				

April
S	M	T	W	T	F	S
			1	2	3	4
5	6	7	8	9	10	11
12	13	14	15	16	17	18
19	20	21	22	23	24	25
26	27	28	29	30		

May
S	M	T	W	T	F	S
					1	2
3	4	5	6	7	8	9
10	11	12	13	14	15	16
17	18	19	20	21	22	23
24	25	26	27	28	29	30
31						

June
S	M	T	W	T	F	S
	1	2	3	4	5	6
7	8	9	10	11	12	13
14	15	16	17	18	19	20
21	22	23	24	25	26	27
28	29	30				

July
S	M	T	W	T	F	S
			1	2	3	4
5	6	7	8	9	10	11
12	13	14	15	16	17	18
19	20	21	22	23	24	25
26	27	28	29	30	31	

August
S	M	T	W	T	F	S
						1
2	3	4	5	6	7	8
9	10	11	12	13	14	15
16	17	18	19	20	21	22
23	24	25	26	27	28	29
30	31					

September
S	M	T	W	T	F	S
		1	2	3	4	5
6	7	8	9	10	11	12
13	14	15	16	17	18	19
20	21	22	23	24	25	26
27	28	29	30			

October
S	M	T	W	T	F	S
				1	2	3
4	5	6	7	8	9	10
11	12	13	14	15	16	17
18	19	20	21	22	23	24
25	26	27	28	29	30	31

November
S	M	T	W	T	F	S
1	2	3	4	5	6	7
8	9	10	11	12	13	14
15	16	17	18	19	20	21
22	23	24	25	26	27	28
29	30					

December
S	M	T	W	T	F	S
		1	2	3	4	5
6	7	8	9	10	11	12
13	14	15	16	17	18	19
20	21	22	23	24	25	26
27	28	29	30	31		

Taurus Daily Horoscope 2026

The time zone is America Eastern Time,
EST or EDT during daylight saving time.

In the realm of astrology, the differences between various horoscope books for each zodiac sign stem from the intricate tapestry of celestial activity constantly unfolding in the skies. As your astrologer, my approach is to hone in on the pivotal aspects affecting a specific star sign on any given day, recognizing the uniqueness inherent in each zodiac entity.

Crafting horoscopes demands a discerning focus on the predominant astrological influences directly shaping the experiences of a particular sign. While multiple planetary configurations may be at play, I prioritize the astrological aspects that carry greater significance for a specific zodiac sign.

Delving into the ruling planets, houses, and elemental attributes associated with each sign further enriches the depth of my interpretations. This meticulous attention ensures that the guidance provided resonates authentically with the distinctive characteristics and tendencies of the intended audience.

The objective is to deliver personalized insights and advice grounded in the cosmic dynamics relevant to each zodiac sign. By emphasizing the most impactful astrological facets, I aim to assist readers in comprehending themselves more profoundly and navigating the energies surrounding them. By embracing the strengths, challenges, and opportunities inherent in each zodiac sign, my horoscope book endeavors to offer a tailored and insightful roadmap for self-discovery and growth.

Crystal

"The starry vault of heaven is in truth the open book of cosmic projection…"

—Carl Jung

JANUARY

Mon	Tue	Wed	Thu	Fri	Sat	Sun
			1	2	3	4
5	6	7	8	9	10	11
12	13	14	15	16	17	18
19	20	21	22	23	24	25
26	27	28	29	30	31	

NEW MOON

_____

_____

_____

_____

_____

_____

_____

_____

_____

_____

_____

_____

_____

_____

_____

_____

_____

_____

_____

_____

WOLF MOON

29 Monday

As the Moon gracefully transitions into Taurus, you may sense a shift towards a more grounded and stable emotional state. This astrological transition encourages you to seek comfort and security in your surroundings. Taurus' energy fosters a desire for simplicity, physical pleasures, and a connection to the natural world. During this time, you might find solace in sensory experiences like good food, music, or spending time in nature.

30 Tuesday

Mercury square Saturn. You may face obstacles when expressing your thoughts and ideas, as Saturn's restrictive energy can inhibit the free flow of Mercury's communication. This aspect may make you prone to self-doubt and critical self-talk, causing you to second-guess your abilities and ideas. However, it also endows you with a disciplined and structured mind, allowing you to excel in tasks that require precision and attention to detail.

31 Wednesday

As the Moon enters Gemini on New Year's Eve, you may notice a noticeable shift in your emotional energy and social interactions. Gemini is an air sign associated with curiosity, communication, and versatility. This lunar transition can inspire you to seek out lively conversations and engage in stimulating activities to ring in the new year. Your mood may become light-hearted, making connecting with various people at celebratory gatherings easier.

1 Thursday

The Sun Trine South Node at 5:22 AM indicates a harmonious integration of past experiences and wisdom into your present life. This aspect suggests that you're able to draw upon insights gained from your history with ease and confidence. You may find yourself naturally embodying the strengths and lessons learned from previous chapters. It's a time to honor the valuable contributions of your past while embracing the opportunities for evolution that lie ahead.

2 Friday

At 8:09 AM, the Moon ingresses into Cancer, emphasizing emotional sensitivity, nurturing instincts, and a desire for security in your surroundings. Cancer is the sign ruled by the Moon, so its ingress enhances your emotional receptivity and heightens your need for comfort and familiarity. During this lunar transit, you may find yourself more attuned to the needs of loved ones and seeking solace in domestic activities. Engage in activities that evoke emotional nourishment.

3 Saturday

At 5:04 AM, a Full Moon graces the sky, illuminating emotions and bringing a culmination of energies initiated during the previous lunar cycle. Full Moons represent a time of heightened emotions, clarity, and culmination. It's a potent period for releasing what no longer serves you and embracing transformation. You may experience a surge of emotions or insights, highlighting areas of your life that require attention or closure. Use this time to release baggage or issues.

4 Sunday

The Moon ingresses into Leo, infusing the atmosphere with warmth, creativity, and self-expression. This lunar transit encourages you to embrace your inner fire, passion, and individuality. You may feel a desire for recognition, attention, and creative expression. It's a favorable period for engaging in activities that bring you joy, pursuing your passions, and showcasing your unique talents. Embrace Leo's playful and expressive energy to ignite your creativity and fuel your inner spark.

5 Monday

With Mercury in Capricorn transiting your ninth house, your approach to higher learning, travel, and philosophical exploration becomes more focused and goal-oriented. This period encourages you to pursue intellectual and spiritual growth with a disciplined and strategic mindset. You may find yourself more willing to engage in activities that require careful planning and organization. This is a time to channel your mental energy into expanding your horizons.

6 Tuesday

At 11:56 AM, the Moon gracefully transitions into Virgo, marking a shift towards practicality and organization. Emotionally, the Virgo Moon encourages introspection and a desire for orderliness in your inner world. You may find solace in routines, rituals, and practical activities that promote a sense of stability and well-being. Take this opportunity to assess your goals, streamline your daily routines, and attend to tasks that require your attention with diligence and care.

7 Wednesday

With Mercury in Capricorn transiting your ninth house, your approach to higher learning, travel, and philosophical exploration becomes more disciplined and strategic. You may find yourself focusing on practical ways to expand your knowledge and explore new horizons. This period encourages you to embrace a systematic approach to intellectual and spiritual growth, blending your ambitious nature with clear and effective communication.

8 Thursday

The Moon gracefully transitions into Libra, encouraging you to seek balance, harmony, and cooperation in your relationships and surroundings. During this lunar transit, you find yourself drawn to activities that promote peace, beauty, and social connection. Use this time to cultivate harmony in your interactions, prioritize diplomacy, and appreciate the beauty in your environment. The nurturing energy of Libra creates equilibrium, ensuring that you feel supported.

9 Friday

Venus opposes Jupiter, presenting a celestial dance between love, pleasure, and expansion. This aspect can bring about a sense of optimism in matters related to relationships, finances, and personal values. However, there is a risk of overindulgence, so it's important to maintain moderation in your pursuits. By embracing a sense of gratitude and tempering your desires with wisdom, you can harness the positive energy of this alignment to cultivate meaningful experiences.

10 Saturday

Mars opposes Jupiter, intensifying the energy of ambition, assertiveness, and drive. This aspect can ignite a strong urge to take action and pursue your goals with vigor. However, there's also a potential for impulsiveness or reckless behavior under this influence. It's crucial to channel this energy productively, focusing on projects or endeavors that align with your long-term vision and values. Strive to harness the expansive power of Jupiter constructively.

11 Sunday

The Moon gracefully transitions into Scorpio, infusing your emotions with intensity, depth, and a desire for transformation. Scorpio's influence encourages you to embrace vulnerability, confront your fears, and release what no longer serves you. Use this time to engage in introspection, uncover hidden motivations, and heal emotional wounds. Trust in your intuition and allow yourself to undergo profound inner growth as you navigate the enigmatic waters of Scorpio.

12 Monday

A new chapter brings beneficial options, painting a brighter picture of what's possible when you stay open to curious leads. Lunar energies encourage improvement at the core of upcoming changes, launching an exciting direction filled with opportunities. Something special may make a grand entrance, kicking off a journey of inspiration and exhilaration, encouraging you to take on new endeavors that stimulate creativity and cultivate your talents.

13 Tuesday

At 6:34 PM, the Moon gracefully enters Sagittarius, ushering in a period characterized by enthusiasm, optimism, and a thirst for adventure. During this lunar transit, you may feel a strong urge to explore new horizons, expand your knowledge, and embrace a spirit of freedom and spontaneity. Sagittarius encourages you to seek meaning and inspiration through travel, higher learning, and cultural experiences.

14 Wednesday

At 3:17 AM, Mercury opposes Jupiter, creating a dynamic interplay between communication, intellect, and expansion. This aspect can amplify your thoughts, ideas, and beliefs, leading to enthusiastic discussions, expansive thinking, and a desire to explore new horizons. You may feel inspired to share your knowledge, express your opinions, or embark on intellectual pursuits that broaden your understanding of the world.

15 Thursday

Venus trines Uranus, introducing an element of excitement, spontaneity, and innovation into your love life and creative endeavors. This aspect encourages you to embrace change, explore new possibilities, and break free from old patterns. You may feel drawn to unconventional experiences that bring a sense of freedom and excitement. Overall, this aspect encourages you to embrace the unexpected and welcome positive shifts in your relationships and artistic pursuits.

16 Friday

The Moon gracefully transitions into Capricorn, marking a time of increased focus, determination, and practicality. During this lunar transit, you may feel more disciplined, organized, and goal-oriented in your approach to life. Capricorn's influence encourages you to take responsibility for your emotions and actions and prioritize long-term success. Use this time to set clear objectives, establish structures and routines, and pursue goals with unwavering dedication.

17 Saturday

At 5:41 AM, the Sun sextiles Saturn, bringing a sense of stability, discipline, and practicality to your endeavors. This aspect encourages you to take a structured approach to your goals, honoring commitments and laying down solid foundations for future success. Use this time to focus on long-term planning, establish boundaries, and demonstrate leadership through responsible action. It's a fantastic time for planning and growth in your life.

18 Sunday

At 2:53 PM, a New Moon graces the sky, marking the beginning of a new lunar cycle and offering a fresh start in manifesting your intentions and aspirations. It is a potent time for setting goals, planting seeds of intention, and envisioning the path ahead. Embrace the energy of renewal and possibility as you embark on a journey of growth and transformation under the darkened skies. Allow the whispers of the universe to guide you towards your dreams.

19 Monday

The Sun sextiles Neptune and blends imagination, spirituality, and compassion with a touch of magic and inspiration. This aspect invites you to tap into your intuition, connect with your inner wisdom, and pursue creative endeavors that uplift the soul. Embrace the beauty of dreams, find solace in the depths of your imagination, and be guided by the gentle flow of inspiration. Trust in the power of faith and surrender as you navigate the mysteries of the unseen.

20 Tuesday

At 12:56 AM, Mars trines Uranus, infusing you with boldness, drive, and a willingness to break free from constraints. This aspect ignites your passion for change and encourages you to take decisive action toward your goals with courage and confidence. Embrace your inner rebel and harness the revolutionary energy of Mars and Uranus to pursue your aspirations fearlessly and with determination.

21 Wednesday

The Moon gracefully transitions into Pisces, infusing the atmosphere with sensitivity, intuition, and compassion. During this lunar transit, you may experience a heightened connection to your emotions, dreams, and the unseen realms. Pisces' influence encourages you to embrace creativity and spiritual exploration. Allow yourself to flow with the gentle currents of intuition and imagination, finding solace in moments of introspection and divine connection.

22 Thursday

Mercury in Aquarius in the tenth house enhances your ability to pursue career success with innovation and determination. You may feel more driven to achieve professional goals through clear and well-organized efforts. It is a time to approach your career with a practical and systematic mindset, allowing new ideas to bring about significant professional growth. Embrace this opportunity to refine your career strategies and create a lasting impact in your field.

23 Friday

Mars enters Aquarius, initiating a period of innovation, idealism, and collective activism. During this transition, your actions are fueled by a desire for progress. Embrace your role as a visionary thinker and catalyst for transformation, advocating for unconventional solutions and embracing diversity in your pursuits. Step into the realm of progressive thought, where individuality merges with collective vision, sparking innovation and paving the way for societal evolution.

24 Saturday

With the celestial bodies casting a favorable light, the path ahead is brimming with exciting choices and decisions, helping you navigate past previous obstacles and embrace transformation. As you venture into uncharted territories, invitations to explore will bring a sense of lightness and momentum to your journey. Engaging with like-minded individuals will rejuvenate your spirit and renew your surroundings.

25 Sunday

The Moon gracefully transitions into Taurus, grounding you in a sense of stability, comfort, and practicality. This lunar ingress invites you to indulge in sensory pleasures, cultivate a sense of security, and appreciate the beauty of the natural world. Embrace moments of relaxation, savor the simple joys of life, and nurture yourself with luxurious comforts. Allow the nurturing energy of Taurus to guide you towards a more profound sense of contentment and well-being.

26 Monday

Neptune gracefully transitions into Aries, marking a significant shift in the collective consciousness towards individuality, independence, and self-discovery. During this transit, the dreamy and ethereal energy of Neptune blends with the bold and assertive qualities of Aries, inspiring innovation, courage, and pioneering spirit. Embrace this cosmic alignment as an opportunity to explore new horizons, break from limitations, and pursue your dreams with unwavering determination.

27 Tuesday

The Moon in Gemini infuses the atmosphere with a light, curious, and adaptable energy. During this lunar transit, you may find yourself more inclined towards socializing, communication, and intellectual pursuits. Gemini's influence encourages you to embrace variety, exchange ideas, and engage in lively conversations with others. Use this time to explore new interests, connect with diverse perspectives, and remain open to the ever-changing flow of experiences.

28 Wednesday

As Venus moves through Aquarius in your tenth house, you may feel inspired to pursue career paths that are unconventional or ahead of their time. Embrace the opportunity to break free from traditional career norms and explore new avenues that align with your values and aspirations. This transit is a time to trust your intuition and follow your passion, knowing that your unique approach can lead to professional success and fulfillment.

29 Thursday

At 5:31 PM, the Moon tenderly transitions into Cancer, ushering in a period of emotional sensitivity, nurturing energy, and introspection. During this lunar transit, you may find yourself drawn to the comforts of home, seeking solace in familiar surroundings and prioritizing the needs of loved ones. Cancer's influence encourages you to honor your feelings, nurture your emotional well-being, and cultivate a sense of security and belonging.

FEBRUARY

Mon	Tue	Wed	Thu	Fri	Sat	Sun
						1
2	3	4	5	6	7	8
9	10	11	12	13	14	15
16	17	18	19	20	21	22
23	24	25	26	27	28	

New Moon

_____

_____

_____

_____

_____

_____

_____

_____

_____

_____

_____

_____

_____

_____

_____

_____

_____

_____

SNOW MOON

_____

_____

_____

_____

_____

_____

_____

_____

_____

_____

_____

_____

_____

_____

_____

_____

_____

_____

_____

30 Friday

The stars highlight a strong emphasis on spiritual growth and connecting with what moves you on a soul level. This period underscores the importance of improving your circumstances, leading to increased abundance, happiness, and companionship. Emphasis on home and family life, combined with companionship from friends, culminates in a happy period with rising prospects. It creates a positive ripple effect that lays the foundation for future success.

31 Saturday

The Moon majestically enters Leo, infusing the atmosphere with warmth, creativity, and self-expression. During this lunar transit, you may feel a strong desire to shine brightly, express your unique personality, and bask in the spotlight. Leo's influence encourages you to embrace your individuality, celebrate your talents, and pursue activities that bring you joy and fulfillment. Allow yourself to be playful, confident, and unapologetically authentic as you express with passion.

1 Sunday

At 5:10 PM, the Full Moon illuminates the sky, casting its radiant glow and culminating the lunar cycle with a powerful surge of energy and intensity. This phase symbolizes completion, fruition, and the realization of intentions set during the New Moon. It's a time of heightened emotions, revelations, and clarity as the Full Moon brings hidden truths to light and invites you to release what no longer serves you.

2 Monday

The Moon gracefully transitions into Virgo, ushering in a period of practicality, organization, and attention to detail. During this lunar transit, you may feel inclined to focus on tasks that require precision, efficiency, and service to others. Virgo's influence encourages you to attend to practical matters, analyze situations with a critical eye, and strive for perfection in your endeavors. Embrace the earthy energy of Virgo to streamline your routines and improve your productivity.

3 Tuesday

With Uranus now moving direct, you may feel a sense of freedom, excitement, and a renewed desire for progress. Embrace the revolutionary energy of Uranus to break free from old patterns, embrace your authenticity, and boldly pursue your unique path forward. Allow yourself to embrace change with courage and openness, trusting in the universe to guide you toward new experiences and opportunities for growth.

4 Wednesday

Expect many changes that will improve your circumstances and bottom line, generating significant forward momentum. Celestial movements support you as you shift away from outdated patterns, helping you discover hidden blessings in learning and honing your talents. Proactive efforts will pay dividends as you climb to new levels of success in your career. New possibilities open a prosperous path, leading to a time of learning, growth, and productivity.

5 Thursday

The Moon in Libra brings harmony, balance, and interpersonal relationships. During this lunar transit, you feel drawn towards seeking fairness, cooperation, and peace in your interactions with others. Libra's influence encourages you to cultivate diplomacy, empathy, and a willingness to compromise for the sake of mutual understanding. Embrace the energy of Libra to foster harmonious connections, promote justice, and find beauty in the art of compromise.

6 Friday

You may find yourself drawn to creative expression, spiritual insights, and empathy for others. Pisces' Moon influence encourages you to listen to your inner voice, trust your instincts, and explore the realms of the subconscious mind. Embrace the dreamy energy of Pisces to engage in imaginative pursuits, connect with the deeper truths of existence, and communicate with compassion and understanding. Navigate the mysteries of life and tap into the universal wisdom.

7 Saturday

At 2:13 PM, the Moon gracefully transitions into Scorpio, ushering in a period of intensity, depth, and emotional transformation. During this lunar transit, you may find yourself drawn to explore the hidden realms of the psyche, uncovering buried truths and delving into matters of passion and power. Scorpio's influence encourages you to embrace vulnerability, confront your fears, and undergo profound inner healing.

8 Sunday

At 4:48 AM, Venus squares Uranus, creating dynamic and potentially disruptive energy in matters of love, relationships, and finances. This aspect may bring unexpected changes, disruptions, or conflicts that challenge your sense of stability and security. It's essential to remain flexible and open-minded during this time. Uranus encourages you to break free from limiting patterns and embrace authenticity and independence in your relationships and financial decisions.

9 Monday

At 7:44 AM, the Moon reaches its last Quarter phase, marking a crucial point in the lunar cycle for reflection, release, and preparation for the upcoming New Moon. This phase encourages you to evaluate your progress since the New Moon, assess what needs to be released or adjusted, and make any necessary course corrections. It's a time to let go of what no longer serves your highest good, release old patterns or habits, and clear the way for new beginnings.

10 Tuesday

By 5:20 AM, Venus enters Pisces, marking a shift towards compassion, sensitivity, and unconditional love in matters of the heart and aesthetics. During this transit, you may find yourself more attuned to the emotions of others, drawn to acts of kindness, and inspired by beauty in all its forms. Venus in Pisces encourages you to connect with your intuition, explore your dreams and fantasies, and cultivate deep, soulful connections with others.

11 Wednesday

The astrological energy today suggests that an area you've been nurturing is set to blossom, offering ample time for soul-stirring conversations that uplift your mood. Sharing moments with kindred spirits leaves you feeling empowered and ready to tackle unique projects. The current planetary alignments mark a significant chapter, opening a gateway to personal growth and creativity. The information you receive today could unlock an enriching journey.

12 Thursday

By 2:44 PM, the Moon gracefully transitions into Capricorn, infusing the atmosphere with a sense of practicality, discipline, and determination. During this lunar transit, you may feel more focused on your long-term goals, responsibilities, and professional endeavors. Capricorn's influence encourages you to take a structured and strategic approach to achieving success and building a solid foundation for the future.

13 Friday

At 7:37 PM, Saturn gracefully transitions into Aries, marking a significant shift in the cosmic landscape and collective consciousness. As Saturn moves into the fiery and assertive sign of Aries, it brings a focus on individuality, initiative, and self-discovery. This transit prompts you to take a more proactive approach to achieving your goals, asserting your independence, and overcoming challenges with courage and determination.

14 Saturday

With Mars in Aquarius transiting your tenth house, your career and public image are energized with a sense of innovation and determination. You are likely to attract attention for your unique contributions and forward-thinking ideas. This period encourages you to take bold steps in your professional life, pursuing paths that reflect your individuality and vision. Let your originality shine, opening doors to new career opportunities.

15 Sunday

The Moon in Aquarius infuses the atmosphere with innovation, individuality, and a spirit of humanitarianism. During this lunar transit, you may feel a heightened sense of social consciousness, a desire for freedom of expression, and a longing to connect with like-minded individuals who share your vision. Aquarius' influence encourages you to think outside the box and champion causes that promote equality, progress, and collective well-being.

16 Monday

At 4:28 PM, Mercury forms a harmonious trine aspect with Jupiter, creating an expansive and optimistic atmosphere for communication, learning, and intellectual pursuits. This aspect enhances your ability to think big, express yourself with confidence, and seek out opportunities for growth and expansion. Embrace the spirit of curiosity, optimism, and open-mindedness as you engage in conversations, share ideas, and explore new horizons.

17 Tuesday

Venus opposes the South Node, creating tension between relationships, values, and past patterns or karma. This aspect may bring up old issues or dynamics in your relationships that need to be addressed and released. It's a time to reassess your values, boundaries, and commitments in relationships and to let go of anything that no longer aligns with your growth and evolution. Embrace the opportunity to break from outdated relationship patterns and cultivate bonds.

18 Wednesday

The Sun in Pisces marks the beginning of a compassionate, intuitive, and spiritually attuned solar journey. During this transit, Aquarius's energy shifts from the individualistic and goal-oriented focus to the dreamy realm of Pisces. The Sun in Pisces encourages you to explore the depths of your emotions, embrace your intuition, and connect with the universal energies that bind us all. It's a time for compassion, forgiveness, and surrendering to the flow of life.

19 Thursday

The Moon boldly transitions into Aries, infusing the atmosphere with dynamic energy, initiative, and courage. During this lunar transit, you may feel a surge of vitality and enthusiasm, propelling you towards exciting adventures. Aries' influence encourages you to take decisive action and pursue your goals with determination. Embrace the pioneering spirit of Aries as you embrace challenges, ignite your passions, and boldly blaze a trail toward growth and self-discovery.

20 Friday

As Neptune moves through Aries in your twelfth house, you may feel a stronger desire to serve others through compassionate and selfless actions. Embrace the opportunity to channel your energy into helping those in need, fostering a sense of fulfillment and spiritual growth. This period invites you to make a difference quietly and humbly, knowing that your efforts can bring healing and positivity to both yourself and the world around you.

21 Saturday

At 6:31 PM, the Moon gracefully transitions into Taurus, infusing the atmosphere with stability, comfort, and a sense of groundedness. During this lunar transit, you may feel drawn to activities that engage your senses, such as enjoying delicious food, spending time in nature, or indulging in creature comforts. Taurus' influence encourages you to cultivate a sense of security, appreciate the beauty in your surroundings, and honor your physical well-being.

22 Sunday

Venus forms a harmonious trine aspect with Jupiter, ushering in a wave of optimism, abundance, and joy in matters of love, relationships, and finances. This celestial alignment brings blessings and opportunities for growth, expansion, and fulfillment in your personal and romantic life. You may feel more open-hearted, generous, and inclined to enjoy life's pleasures to the fullest during this time. It's a favorable moment for socializing and making meaningful connections.

23 Monday

At 9:29 PM, the Moon gracefully transitions into Gemini, infusing the atmosphere with a sense of curiosity, communication, and versatility. During this lunar transition, you may feel more mentally agile, pleasant, and open to new ideas and experiences. Gemini's influence encourages you to engage in stimulating conversations, pursue intellectual interests, and explore different perspectives. It's a time for learning, networking, and embracing the diversity of life.

24 Tuesday

The Moon reaches its First Quarter phase, marking a crucial point in the lunar cycle for taking action and moving forward with your intentions. This phase invites you to evaluate your progress since the New Moon and make any necessary adjustments to your plans. It's a time to overcome challenges, assert your willpower, and push forward toward your goals with determination. Embrace the energy of the First Quarter Moon to face any obstacles with courage.

25 Wednesday

Venus in Pisces in the eleventh house enhances your ability to connect with like-minded individuals and contribute to community projects with grace and charm. You may feel more driven to achieve long-term social and communal objectives through meaningful and empathetic interactions. It is a time to approach your social endeavors with a balanced and intuitive mindset. Your ability to communicate your ideas with compassion and creativity can lead to progress.

26 Thursday

At 1:47 AM, Mercury turns retrograde, initiating a period of reflection, revision, and reevaluation in communication, travel, and technology. This cosmic event may bring delays, misunderstandings, and glitches in plans or communication. It's a time to slow down, review your decisions and commitments, and make adjustments as needed. Embrace the opportunity to revisit past projects, reconnect with old friends, and reflect on your thoughts and ideas.

MARCH

Mon	Tue	Wed	Thu	Fri	Sat	Sun
						1
2	3	4	5	6	7	8
9	10	11	12	13	14	15
16	17	18	19	20	21	22
23	24	25	26	27	28	29
30	31					

NEW MOON

_____

_____

_____

_____

_____

_____

_____

_____

_____

_____

_____

_____

_____

_____

_____

_____

_____

_____

_____

WORM MOON

_____

_____

_____

_____

_____

_____

_____

_____

_____

_____

_____

_____

_____

_____

_____

_____

_____

_____

_____

27 Friday

Mars squares Uranus, generating a surge of volatile and unpredictable energy in action, assertion, and rebellion. This aspect may bring sudden disruptions, conflicts, or accidents that require flexibility and adaptability to navigate. It's essential to exercise caution and avoid impulsive or reckless behavior under this influence. Channel the dynamic energy of Mars square Uranus into constructive outlets for change and innovation rather than engaging in power struggles.

28 Saturday

The Moon boldly transitions into Leo, infusing the atmosphere with confidence, creativity, and a desire for self-expression. During this lunar transit, you may feel a heightened sense of pride, enthusiasm, and a longing for recognition. Leo's influence encourages you to embrace your unique talents, showcase your creativity, and bask in the spotlight of your authenticity. It's a time for celebrating your individuality and indulging in playful activities.

1 Sunday

With the Sun in Pisces transiting your eleventh house, your focus on friendships and community involvement becomes more intuitive and empathetic. This period encourages you to approach your social life with compassion and understanding. You may find yourself more interested in building connections that are based on shared values and spiritual beliefs. It is a time to channel your energy into cultivating meaningful friendships and contributing to the greater good.

2 Monday

At 7:34 AM, the Moon gracefully transitions into Virgo, infusing the atmosphere with practicality, organization, and attention to detail. During this lunar transit, you may feel inclined to focus on efficiency, productivity, and improving areas of your life that require refinement. Virgo's influence encourages you to analyze situations with clarity, attend to tasks with precision, and strive for perfection in your endeavors. Embrace the earthy energy of Virgo to create order out of chaos.

3 Tuesday

As the Moon reaches its peak in brightness, it invites you to reflect on your intentions set during the New Moon and acknowledge the progress you've made since then. Embrace the illuminating energy of the Full Moon to let go of what no longer serves you, celebrate your achievements, and embrace the transformative power of surrender. Allow the moonlight to guide you as you navigate the currents of change and move forward with a renewed sense of purpose and direction.

4 Wednesday

Venus forms a harmonious sextile aspect with Uranus, infusing your relationships and interactions with excitement, spontaneity, and a sense of adventure. This alignment may bring unexpected encounters, thrilling experiences, or opportunities for growth and liberation in matters of love and creativity. Embrace the innovative energy of Venus sextile Uranus to explore new avenues of expression, break from routine, and enjoy change with openness and enthusiasm.

5 Thursday

At 12:13 PM, the Sun forms a harmonious trine aspect with Jupiter, infusing the atmosphere with optimism, expansion, and abundance. This celestial alignment brings a sense of confidence, growth, and opportunity, encouraging you to embrace your potential and pursue your goals with enthusiasm. It's a favorable time for taking calculated risks, exploring new horizons, and tapping into your inner wisdom and optimism.

6 Friday

The Moon moves into Scorpio, infusing the atmosphere with intensity, depth, and emotional transformation. During this lunar transit, you may find yourself delving into the realms of the subconscious, seeking more profound truths, and exploring hidden aspects of yourself and others. Scorpio's influence encourages you to embrace authenticity, confront your fears, and embrace the power of regeneration and rebirth. Dive into the depths of your emotions, trust your intuition.

7 Saturday

With Mars in Pisces transiting your eleventh house, your approach to social networks and community involvement becomes more intuitive and compassionate. This period encourages you to focus on building deep and meaningful connections within your social circles. You may draw friends and groups that offer spiritual and emotional support. It is a time to channel your energy into creating a sense of unity and shared purpose within your community.

8 Sunday

Sun in Pisces in the eleventh house enhances your ability to connect with like-minded individuals who share your vision and ideals. You may feel more driven to explore new ways of engaging with your community and making a positive impact. Embrace this opportunity to build strong bonds with friends and allies who support your goals and aspirations. Your compassionate approach to social interactions will help you create unity and collaboration within your community.

9 Monday

At 11:36 AM, the Moon transitions into Sagittarius, infusing the atmosphere with a sense of adventure, optimism, and exploration. During this lunar transit, you may feel a strong desire for freedom, expansion, and philosophical understanding. Sagittarius' influence encourages you to embrace new experiences, broaden your horizons, and seek meaning in the world around you. It's a time for embracing diversity, learning from different cultures, and expanding your perspective.

10 Tuesday

At 11:36 PM, Jupiter turns direct after a period of retrograde motion, heralding a shift in energy towards expansion, growth, and opportunity. With Jupiter moving forward again, you can expect an increase in optimism, abundance, and forward momentum. This planetary shift encourages you to pursue your goals with confidence, explore new horizons, and embrace the potential for growth and prosperity. Trust in the universe to guide you toward abundance and fulfillment.

11 Wednesday

At 5:39 AM, the Moon reaches its Last Quarter phase, marking a pivotal moment in the lunar cycle for reflection, release, and reassessment. This lunar aspect prompts you to take stock of your progress since the New Moon and evaluate any challenges or obstacles that may be hindering your growth. It's a time to let go of what no longer serves you, release outdated patterns or beliefs, and make space for new beginnings to emerge.

12 Thursday

The Moon gracefully transitions into Capricorn, infusing the atmosphere with a sense of responsibility, ambition, and practicality. During this lunar transit, you may feel more focused on your long-term goals, career aspirations, and commitments. Capricorn's influence encourages you to take a disciplined approach to achieving success, prioritize your responsibilities, and work diligently towards your ambitions. It's a favorable time for planning and organization.

13 Friday

At 4:52 PM, Mars forms an opposition with the South Node, creating a dynamic and potentially challenging aspect that highlights themes of karma, past actions, and release. This alignment may bring forth conflicts, tensions, or confrontations that stem from unresolved issues or patterns from the past. You may find yourself facing resistance or setbacks as you attempt to move forward or experiencing a sense of frustration as old wounds resurface.

14 Saturday

At 11:13 AM, the Moon gracefully transitions into Aquarius, infusing the atmosphere with innovation, uniqueness, and a desire for social connection. During this lunar transit, you may feel a heightened sense of independence, humanitarianism, and intellectual curiosity. Aquarius' influence encourages you to embrace your individuality, think outside the box, and seek out unconventional solutions to challenges. It's a favorable time for engaging in group activities.

15 Sunday

Venus in Aries in the twelfth house enhances your ability to navigate your inner world with boldness and creativity. You may feel more driven to achieve long-term spiritual and psychological objectives through decisive actions. This is a time to approach your inner journey with a proactive and determined mindset. Your ability to communicate your inner experiences and take the lead in spiritual practices can lead to significant progress and enlightenment.

16 Monday

At 7:15 PM, the Moon gracefully transitions into Pisces, infusing the atmosphere with sensitivity, intuition, and imagination. During this lunar transit, you may feel more attuned to your emotions, dreams, and the subtle energies of the universe. Pisces' influence encourages you to embrace your compassionate nature, explore your inner world, and tap into your creativity. It's a favorable time for introspection, meditation, and artistic expression.

17 Tuesday

At 5:00 PM, Mercury forms an opposition aspect with the South Node, creating tension between your current thoughts, communication style, and past patterns or karmic influences. This aspect may bring up challenges related to outdated beliefs, communication issues, or unresolved issues from the past. You may find yourself revisiting old conversations, misunderstandings, or decisions that need to be addressed and released.

18 Wednesday

The New Moon graces the sky, marking the beginning of a new lunar cycle and offering a powerful opportunity for intention setting and new beginnings. This celestial event symbolizes a time of fresh starts, clarity, and manifestation. Set intentions, plant seeds of growth, and open yourself up to the possibilities that lie ahead. Embrace the transformative energy of the New Moon to align your desires with your actions and step into the next phase of your journey with confidence.

19 Thursday

At 12:03 AM, the Moon confidently enters Aries, infusing the atmosphere with dynamic energy, assertiveness, and a pioneering spirit. During this lunar transit, you may feel a surge of motivation, courage, and independence. Aries' influence encourages you to take initiative, embrace challenges head-on, and assert your individuality. It's a favorable time for starting new projects, taking decisive action, and pursuing your goals with enthusiasm.

March

20 Friday

At precisely 10:48 AM, the Sun gracefully enters Aries, heralding the astrological New Year and initiating a new zodiac cycle. Aries, the first sign of the zodiac, infuses the atmosphere with energy, enthusiasm, and a pioneering spirit. It's a time for bold initiatives, fresh starts, and taking decisive action towards your goals. Embrace the fiery energy of Aries as you embrace opportunities for growth, assert your individuality, and pursue your passions with courage and determination.

21 Saturday

Mars forms a harmonious trine aspect with Jupiter, amplifying your confidence, energy, and enthusiasm for taking action. This aspect imbues you with a sense of optimism, courage, and motivation to pursue your goals with vigor and determination. You may feel a surge of vitality and a willingness to take risks or explore new opportunities for growth and expansion. Embrace the dynamic energy of Mars trine Jupiter as you channel your passions into purposeful action.

22 Sunday

Mercury forms an opposition aspect with the South Node, creating tension between your current thought patterns, communication style, and past karmic influences. This aspect may bring up challenges related to outdated beliefs, habitual thinking, or unresolved issues from the past. You may find yourself confronted with misunderstandings, miscommunications, or revisiting old conflicts or patterns. It's essential to approach communication with mindfulness.

23 Monday

At 4:18 AM, the Moon gracefully transitions into Gemini, infusing the atmosphere with a sense of curiosity, adaptability, and socialization. During this lunar transit, you may feel more inclined to engage in lively conversations, connect with others through communication, and explore a variety of interests and ideas. Gemini's influence encourages you to embrace versatility, intellectual stimulation, and flexibility in your interactions and pursuits.

24 Tuesday

Improvement looms overhead as a new influence brings choice opportunities. Cosmic forces reshuffle the decks of potential and offer a unique journey forward. It feeds your spirit with inspiration as you embark on developing new possibilities. Curiosity, guided by celestial energies, points you in the right direction. Life becomes more accessible, expansive, and progressive. Developments ahead help you overcome barriers and reach a new level of prosperity.

25 Wednesday

At 2:16 PM, the Sun forms a harmonious sextile aspect with Pluto, deepening your sense of personal power, transformation, and regeneration. This aspect brings opportunities for self-discovery, empowerment, and growth as you delve into the depths of your psyche and uncover hidden truths. You may feel more capable of overcoming obstacles, releasing old patterns, and embracing positive change in your life.

26 Thursday

A fresh cycle beckons and helps you move toward new possibilities. Astrological energies give you the green light to cultivate change by working with your creativity and nurturing your talents. Clear skies breeze into your life, bringing curious options to explore. New leads emerge that help you make the most of your abilities, activating a prosperous chapter of growing security and stability in your life. The universe supports your journey, making this a time of fruitful exploration.

27 Friday

At 10:10 AM, the Moon gracefully transitions into Leo, infusing the atmosphere with warmth, creativity, and a desire for self-expression. During this lunar transit, you may feel more outgoing, confident, and eager to shine in the spotlight. Leo's influence encourages you to embrace your unique talents, passions, and individuality and to share your light with the world. Allow yourself to bask in the glow of self-assurance and let your inner radiance illuminate your path forward.

28 Saturday

At 6:10 PM, Saturn forms a harmonious sextile aspect with Pluto, bringing stability, transformation, and empowerment to the forefront. This rare and potent alignment combines the disciplined energy of Saturn with the regenerative power of Pluto, offering an opportunity for profound growth and positive change. You may find yourself more capable of overcoming challenges, restructuring your life, and achieving long-term goals with patience and determination.

29 Sunday

At 3:33 PM, the Moon gracefully transitions into Virgo, bringing a shift towards practicality, organization, and attention to detail. During this lunar transit, you may feel inclined to focus on efficiency, productivity, and improving your daily routines. Virgo's influence encourages you to pay attention to the finer details of life, attend to tasks with precision, and strive for perfection in your endeavors. It's a favorable time for analyzing problems and implementing solutions.

APRIL

Mon	Tue	Wed	Thu	Fri	Sat	Sun
		1	2	3	4	5
6	7	8	9	10	11	12
13	14	15	16	17	18	19
20	21	22	23	24	25	26
27	28	29	30			

NEW MOON

_____

_____

_____

_____

_____

_____

_____

_____

_____

_____

_____

_____

_____

_____

_____

_____

_____

_____

_____

_____

Pink Moon

_____

_____

_____

_____

_____

_____

_____

_____

_____

_____

_____

_____

_____

_____

_____

_____

_____

_____

_____

30 Monday

Venus gracefully enters Taurus, marking a shift in the cosmic landscape towards indulgence, sensuality, and earthly delights. This celestial event invites you to revel in life's pleasures, savoring the beauty of the natural world and cultivating a deeper appreciation for the finer things. Under the influence of Taurus, Venus encourages you to nurture your senses, indulge in luxurious comforts, and create a harmonious environment that satisfies both your physical and emotional needs.

31 Tuesday

The Moon gracefully transitions into Libra, ushering in a period of harmony, diplomacy, and social grace. During this lunar transit, you may feel a heightened desire for balance and fairness in your interactions with others. Libra's influence encourages you to seek compromise, find common ground, and prioritize cooperation in your relationships. It's a favorable time for socializing, networking, and fostering connections with others based on mutual respect and understanding.

1 Wednesday

At 10:13 PM, the Full Moon graces the sky, heralding a moment of culmination and illumination in the lunar cycle. This celestial event invites you to celebrate achievements, acknowledge progress, and release. Emotions may run high, and insights may surface, urging you to pay attention to your dreams, intuition, and inner guidance. Embrace the transformative energy of the Full Moon as you surrender to its wisdom and embrace cycles of growth and renewal in your life.

2 Thursday

With Mercury in Pisces transiting your eleventh house, your approach to social networks and community involvement becomes more intuitive and imaginative. This period encourages you to build meaningful connections and actively pursue your aspirations with a compassionate and visionary mindset. You may find yourself more willing to engage in group activities that require a holistic and empathetic approach.

3 Friday

At 7:30 AM, Mercury forms a harmonious trine aspect with Jupiter, amplifying mental clarity, expansive thinking, and the potential for positive communication and learning. This alignment encourages you to embrace optimism, broaden your perspective, and engage in meaningful discussions that inspire growth and understanding. It's a favorable time for exploring new ideas, pursuing higher knowledge, and sharing your insights with others.

4 Saturday

With the Sun in Aries transiting your twelfth house, your focus on introspection, spirituality, and inner growth becomes more intense and proactive. This period encourages you to take an active role in exploring your inner world and addressing hidden fears and insecurities. You may feel more driven to engage in spiritual practices and seek out experiences that promote healing and self-discovery. This is a time to channel your energy into inner work and personal transformation.

5 Sunday

At 6:22 PM, the Sun forms a challenging square aspect with Jupiter, creating a dynamic and expansive energy that can lead to both opportunities and challenges. This alignment may bring about a sense of optimism, enthusiasm, and a desire for growth and expansion. However, there is also a risk of overconfidence, excessive optimism, or taking on too much at once. It's essential to balance ambition with practicality and avoid overcommitting to unrealistic goals or ventures.

APRIL

6 Monday

The Venus trine with the South Node indicates a harmonious integration of past experiences and lessons learned into your present relationships and values. You may find yourself embodying the wisdom gained from previous connections, allowing you to move with greater clarity and authenticity. Embrace the balancing energy of this aspect as you navigate your relationships and align with your higher purpose, guided by the wisdom of both past and present experiences.

7 Tuesday

Breaking free from limitations and expanding your life brings unique adventures that reveal a journey blossoming into a meaningful path forward. The stars craft your vision for future growth, promoting an environment that nurtures your talents. You advance life forward and develop your skills in a new area, continuously evolving. Broadening your horizons under the guidance of cosmic influences offers an uplifting trajectory that connects with unique opportunities.

8 Wednesday

At 12:11 PM, Mars forms a harmonious sextile aspect with Uranus, igniting a surge of energy, innovation, and spontaneity. This aspect encourages you to embrace change, take risks, and assert yourself boldly in pursuit of your goals. You may find yourself inspired to break free from routine, experiment with new approaches, or initiate exciting projects that push the boundaries of what's possible. A surge of confidence lets you step outside of your comfort zone.

9 Thursday

At 3:39 PM, Mars boldly enters Aries, its home sign, marking the beginning of a dynamic and assertive phase. This celestial shift ignites a surge of energy and drive, propelling you towards action and initiative. With Mars in Aries, you're infused with a sense of courage, passion, and determination, ready to pursue your goals with enthusiasm. This transit encourages you to embrace challenges, assert your individuality, and fearlessly step into leadership roles.

10 Friday

At 7:55 PM, the Moon gracefully transitions into Aquarius, infusing the atmosphere with innovative, progressive, and humanitarian energy. During this lunar transit, you may feel inclined towards individuality, originality, and social connectivity. Aquarius' influence encourages us to embrace our uniqueness, think outside the box, and collaborate with others to bring about positive change. It's a time for embracing diversity and exploring unconventional ideas.

11 Saturday

With Venus in Taurus transiting your first house, your charm and attractiveness are enhanced by a grounded and sensual energy. You may find yourself exuding a serene and magnetic aura that draws others to you. This period encourages you to embrace a steady and reliable approach to self-expression, blending your natural charm with a desire for stability and comfort. Your increased magnetism can make a strong impression.

12 Sunday

Sun in Aries in the twelfth house enhances your desire to explore the depths of your soul and connect with your inner self. You may find yourself more willing to confront your shadows and embrace the process of healing and transformation. Embrace this opportunity to engage in practices such as meditation, dream work, and spiritual retreats that facilitate inner growth. Your assertive approach to introspection will help you release old patterns.

13 Monday

The Pisces' Moon influence encourages you to connect with your inner world, explore your dreams, and tap into your creative and spiritual depths. Under this lunar transit, you may find yourself more attuned to the subtle energies around you, seeking solace in artistic expression or engaging in acts of compassion and empathy. Embrace the gentle power of the Pisces Moon as you nurture your soul, explore your inner landscapes, and find beauty in the realm of the imagination.

14 Tuesday

At 11:23 PM, Mercury makes its ingress into Aries, infusing the realm of communication with boldness, assertiveness, and spontaneity. As Mercury enters this fiery sign, you may notice a shift in your communication style, becoming more direct, assertive, and action-oriented. Your thoughts and ideas may take on a sense of urgency, motivating you to take swift action and pursue your goals with passion and determination.

15 Wednesday

The Moon in Aries ignites a surge of initiative, passion, and assertiveness. This lunar ingress marks a time of dynamic energy and enthusiasm, urging you to take decisive action and pursue your goals with courage and determination. Under the influence of Aries, you may feel more confident, independent, and eager to embrace new challenges head-on. It's a favorable time for starting new projects, asserting your individuality, and embracing a sense of adventure.

16 Thursday

At 2:55 PM, Mars forms a harmonious sextile aspect with Pluto, aligning the energies of action and transformation powerfully and constructively. This celestial event infuses you with determination, resilience, and the drive to make significant progress towards your goals. Under this influence, you possess the courage and strength to overcome obstacles, break through limitations, and assert yourself with confidence and assertiveness.

17 Friday

The Moon gracefully transitions into Taurus, grounding the energy of the day with stability, sensuality, and a focus on material comfort and security. In Taurus, you are invited to slow down, savor the present moment, and nurture yourself and your surroundings with care and appreciation. This lunar ingress encourages you to connect with nature, indulge in life's simple pleasures, and cultivate a sense of stability and abundance in your life.

18 Saturday

Today, you can penetrate beneath the surface and gain profound insights into yourself and others. It's a favorable time for research, investigation, and psychological exploration, as well as for having meaningful conversations that lead to personal growth and transformation. Embrace the transformative energy of Mercury sextile Pluto as you engage in deep, honest communication and harness the power of your intellect to create positive change in your life.

19 Sunday

At 9:41 PM, the Sun enters your sign, marking the beginning of Taurus season and grounding the energy in stability, sensuality, and practicality. In Taurus, the Sun invites you to slow down, appreciate life's simple pleasures, and connect with the physical world. It's a time for cultivating abundance, enjoying creature comforts, and nurturing your sense of security. Embrace the earthy energy of the Taurus season as you focus on building a solid foundation for your goals.

APRIL

20 Monday

With Mercury in Aries transiting your twelfth house, your approach to introspection and spirituality becomes more dynamic and assertive. This period encourages you to explore your inner world and address subconscious issues with a confident and proactive approach. You may find yourself more willing to engage in activities that require a straightforward mindset. This is a time to channel your mental energy into creating inner strength and profound self-discovery.

21 Tuesday

In Cancer, the Moon encourages you to prioritize your feelings, connect with your innermost needs, and seek comfort and reassurance from loved ones. You may find yourself more attuned to the needs of others and inclined to nurture and care for those around you. It's a favorable time for creating a safe and supportive home environment, spending quality time with family, and honoring your emotional well-being.

22 Wednesday

With Mars in Aries transiting your twelfth house, your approach to introspection and spirituality becomes more assertive and transformative. This period encourages you to take bold steps in exploring your inner world and addressing subconscious fears. You may find yourself more willing to confront hidden issues and push for profound spiritual growth. This is a time to channel your energy into practices that promote inner strength and self-discovery.

23 Thursday

The Moon's First Quarter phase is a pivotal point that encourages you to take initiative, overcome challenges, and move forward with determination toward your goals. It's a time for making decisions, taking decisive action, and stepping out of your comfort zone in pursuit of your dreams. Embrace the dynamic energy of the First Quarter Moon as you harness your inner strength and courage to manifest your intentions and propel yourself towards success.

24 Friday

In Gemini, Venus encourages you to explore diverse interests, engage in stimulating conversations, and seek out new experiences. You may find yourself drawn to intellectual pursuits, social gatherings, and opportunities for networking and communication. This transit stimulates your curiosity and appreciation for different perspectives, making it an ideal time for learning, socializing, and enjoying the diversity of life.

25 Saturday

Uranus enters expressive Gemini, initiating a period marked by intellectual stimulation, curiosity, and innovation. Uranus in Gemini encourages you to embrace change, experiment with new ideas, and break free from mental constraints. This transit may spark unexpected insights, sudden shifts in perspective, and opportunities for intellectual growth and liberation. Embrace the dynamic energy of Uranus in Gemini as you explore the vast realm of possibilities.

26 Sunday

Mercury squares Jupiter, creating a dynamic alignment that challenges you to find the balance between optimism and practicality in your communication and thinking processes. This aspect may exaggerate tendencies towards overconfidence, exaggeration, or overestimation of one's abilities. It's essential to avoid hasty decisions or taking on more than you can handle. Instead, strive to maintain a realistic perspective and approach challenges with open-mindedness.

27 Monday

The trine with the South Node indicates a harmonious integration of past experiences, wisdom, and talents into your present life. This aspect suggests that you have the opportunity to draw upon your past achievements, lessons learned, and innate abilities to support your current endeavors. You may find yourself naturally embodying the strengths and qualities developed through previous experiences, allowing you to navigate challenges with ease and grace.

28 Tuesday

Venus forms a harmonious trine aspect with Pluto, creating a potent alignment of love, transformation, and intensity. This celestial event brings depth and passion to your relationships and creative endeavors, allowing you to experience profound emotional connections and transformative experiences. Under this influence, you may feel a deepening of intimacy, a desire for soulful connections, and a willingness to confront and overcome any obstacles to love and personal growth.

29 Wednesday

Venus forms a challenging square aspect with the North Node that indicates potential friction between your current desires and your soul's evolutionary direction. You may feel torn between pursuing immediate pleasures and aligning with your long-term spiritual growth. It's essential to discern whether your choices are in alignment with your higher purpose and make adjustments as needed to honor your soul's journey.

30 Thursday

In Scorpio, the Moon encourages you to delve beneath the surface, confront your innermost desires, and embrace the mysteries of the subconscious mind. You may find yourself experiencing heightened emotional sensitivity and a need for authenticity and intimacy in your interactions with others. This lunar transit invites you to embrace vulnerability, explore your deepest passions, and undergo profound inner healing and rebirth.

MAY

Mon	Tue	Wed	Thu	Fri	Sat	Sun
				1	2	3
4	5	6	7	8	9	10
11	12	13	14	15	16	17
18	19	20	21	22	23	24
25	26	27	28	29	30	31

NEW MOON

FLOWER MOON

MAY

1 Friday

At 2:45 PM, Venus forms a harmonious sextile aspect with Saturn, infusing the day with stability, commitment, and a sense of responsibility in matters of love and finances. This celestial alignment encourages you to build solid foundations in your relationships and investments, fostering long-term security and growth. You may find yourself attracted to mature, reliable partners or drawn to practical, disciplined approaches to your finances.

2 Saturday

Mercury, in your sign, shifts the focus towards practicality, stability, and tangible results. In Taurus, Mercury encourages you to approach matters of the mind with patience, thoroughness, and a systematic approach. Your thinking may become more grounded and deliberate, prioritizing reliability and consistency over spontaneity. This transit favors slow and steady progress, allowing you to carefully consider your words and ideas before expressing them.

3 Sunday

In Sagittarius, the Moon encourages you to embrace a spirit of freedom, exploration, and philosophical inquiry. You may feel a strong desire to break free from routine, seek out new experiences, and broaden your horizons through travel, learning, or spiritual pursuits. This lunar transit ignites your enthusiasm for life, inspiring you to embrace opportunities for growth, discovery, and personal evolution. It's a time for exploring the unknown with confidence and optimism.

MAY

4 Monday

Mars forms a challenging square aspect with Jupiter, marking a time of heightened energy, ambition, and assertiveness, but also potential challenges and conflicts. This celestial alignment can bring about a tendency towards excess, impulsiveness, and overestimation of one's capabilities. You may feel a strong desire to take risks, push boundaries, and pursue your goals with enthusiasm and confidence. However, it's essential to temper your actions with prudence.

5 Tuesday

At 6:08 PM, Mercury forms a challenging square aspect with Pluto, creating an intense and potentially confrontational atmosphere in communication and mental processes. This aspect can bring about power struggles, obsessions, or intense debates that stem from deep-seated issues or hidden truths coming to light. You may encounter resistance or opposition in your interactions, leading to confrontations or a need for psychological insights and transformation.

6 Wednesday

The sextile with the North Node indicates a favorable opportunity to align your thoughts and communication style with your soul's path and higher purpose. You may experience moments of clarity, insight, and synchronicity that guide you toward fulfilling your karmic destiny and spiritual growth. Embrace this cosmic alignment as you engage in meaningful conversations, share your wisdom with others, and pursue knowledge that aligns with your soul's evolutionary journey.

7 Thursday

Venus in Gemini in the second house enhances your ability to attract financial opportunities and manage your resources with creativity and intellect. You may feel more driven to achieve economic stability through social interactions and networking. This is a time to approach your finances with a curious and open-minded mindset. Your ability to value versatility and adaptability in financial matters can lead to increased financial security and satisfaction.

8 Friday

In Aquarius, the Moon encourages you to embrace your uniqueness, express your authentic self, and connect with like-minded individuals who share your vision for the future. You may feel a heightened sense of independence and a desire to break free from conventional norms or restrictions, seeking out experiences that inspire creativity, originality, and social change. This lunar transit sparks a curiosity for new ideas, technologies, and unconventional approaches.

9 Saturday

At 5:11 PM, the Moon reaches its Last Quarter phase, signaling a pivotal moment in the lunar cycle characterized by reflection, reassessment, and release. During this phase, the Moon forms a square aspect with the Sun, creating a tension between the need for closure and the desire to initiate new beginnings. It's a time to take stock of your achievements and challenges since the New Moon and evaluate your progress toward your goals.

10 Sunday

At 10:13 PM, the Sun forms a harmonious sextile aspect with Jupiter, amplifying feelings of optimism, expansion, and abundance. This celestial alignment brings a sense of confidence, enthusiasm, and opportunity, encouraging you to embrace new experiences and broaden your horizons. You may feel a heightened sense of purpose and a greater willingness to take risks or pursue your goals with optimism and faith in the universe.

11 Monday

With Mercury in Taurus transiting your first house, your communication style becomes more grounded and deliberate. This period encourages you to express yourself with clarity and a practical mindset. You may find yourself more focused on conveying your ideas steadily and thoughtfully. This is a time to channel your mental energy into personal projects that benefit from a patient and methodical approach.

12 Tuesday

In Aries, the Moon ignites a fiery energy that inspires you to take decisive action, pursue your goals with enthusiasm, and assert your individuality. You may feel a surge of power and a desire to tackle challenges head-on, fueled by a sense of independence and self-confidence. This lunar transit encourages you to trust your instincts, embrace spontaneity, and fearlessly pursue your passions. It's a favorable time for initiating new projects or embarking on adventures that ignite your spirit.

13 Wednesday

Mercury forms a harmonious sextile aspect with Jupiter, creating a celestial alignment that enhances your mental faculties, communication skills, and intellectual pursuits. This transit brings opportunities for expanded awareness, positive thinking, and learning experiences that broaden your horizons. You may find yourself more open to new ideas, philosophies, or perspectives, eager to explore diverse subjects and engage in stimulating conversations.

14 Thursday

Today, the lunar transit fosters a sense of grounding and contentment, urging you to slow down, appreciate life's pleasures, and cultivate an understanding of gratitude for the abundance that surrounds you. It's a favorable time for creating security in your environment, nurturing your body, and enjoying the fruits of your labor. Embrace the nurturing energy of the Taurus Moon as you reconnect with the earthy pleasures and find solace in the comfort of the present moment.

MAY

15 Friday

Saturn in Aries in the twelfth house enhances your ability to confront and overcome subconscious fears and obstacles with a sense of responsibility and determination. You may feel more focused on engaging in reflective practices and cultivating a deeper connection with your inner self. This is a time to approach your spiritual journey with a structured and systematic mindset. Your ability to persevere through challenges can lead to profound personal growth and healing.

16 Saturday

The New Moon graces the sky, heralding the beginning of a new lunar cycle and offering a powerful opportunity for fresh starts, intentions, and manifestations. This celestial event marks a time of renewal, clarity, and potential, inviting you to set intentions for the future and sow the seeds of your dreams. The New Moon in Gemini encourages you to embrace curiosity, communication, and versatility, inspiring you to explore ideas, connect with others, and adapt to change with ease.

17 Sunday

Mercury in Gemini favors learning, networking, and gathering information from diverse sources, making it ideal for studying, brainstorming, or social activities. Embrace the communicative and adaptable energy of Mercury in Gemini as you embrace the power of curiosity, embrace new opportunities for learning and connection, and explore the world with an open mind and a playful spirit. This transit stimulates your intellect, making you friendly and quick-witted.

18 Monday

In Cancer, Venus encourages you to prioritize emotional connections, family bonds, and domestic harmony. This transit heightens your sensitivity to the needs and feelings of others, fostering a profound sense of empathy and compassion in your relationships. You may feel drawn to create a warm and nurturing environment in your home, surrounded by loved ones and cherished memories. It's a favorable time for expressing love, care, and appreciation to others.

19 Tuesday

Mercury squares both the North Node and the South Node, creating a dynamic tension between your future path and past patterns. The square with the North Node challenges you to align your thoughts and communication with your karmic path and soul's evolution, while the square with the South Node brings attention to habits and beliefs that may hinder your progress. Use this energy to reflect on where you're headed and how past influences may be impacting your trajectory.

20 Wednesday

At 8:39 PM, the Sun gracefully enters Gemini, marking a shift in focus towards communication, versatility, and intellectual exploration. With the Sun in Gemini, curiosity and adaptability are heightened, and there's a greater emphasis on gathering information, engaging in social interactions, and embracing diverse perspectives. This transit encourages you to embrace variety, flexibility, and open-mindedness as you navigate the multifaceted aspects of life.

21 Thursday

With Mercury in Gemini transiting your second house, your approach to finances and material possessions becomes more flexible and innovative. This period encourages you to manage your resources with a focus on versatility and new ideas. You may find yourself more interested in exploring various ways of earning and managing money. It is a time to channel your mental energy into building financial security through creative and adaptable strategies.

22 Friday

Venus forms a challenging square aspect with Neptune, creating a celestial dance that may bring about confusion, idealization, or unrealistic expectations in matters of love, beauty, and finances. This aspect can blur boundaries and lead to misunderstandings or illusions, prompting you to exercise caution in matters of the heart and finances. It's essential to remain grounded and discerning, avoiding making significant decisions based solely on romantic ideals or wishful thinking.

23 Saturday

At 7:12 AM, the Moon reaches its First Quarter phase, marking a significant milestone in the lunar cycle and prompting you to take action towards your goals and intentions set during the New Moon. This lunar phase encourages you to overcome any challenges or obstacles that may arise and to make adjustments as needed to stay on course with your plans. It's a time for decision-making, initiative, and taking concrete steps towards manifesting your desires.

24 Sunday

The Sun forms a harmonious sextile with Neptune, infusing the atmosphere with compassion, intuition, and spiritual insight. This aspect heightens your sensitivity to subtle energies and encourages acts of kindness, empathy, and creative inspiration. You may find yourself more attuned to the needs of others and more receptive to intuitive guidance and artistic inspiration. Use this time to connect with activities that nourish your soul and uplift your spirit.

MAY

25 Monday

The square aspect between the Sun and the lunar nodes encourages you to acknowledge any areas where you may be resisting change or struggling to break free from the past. It's essential to recognize that growth often requires stepping out of your comfort zone and embracing new experiences, even if they feel unfamiliar or challenging. Use this time to reflect on where you may need to let go of old patterns, beliefs, or behaviors that no longer serve your highest good.

26 Tuesday

Mars forms a challenging square aspect with Pluto, intensifying the energy and bringing potential power struggles, conflicts, or confrontations to the surface. This aspect may trigger feelings of frustration, control issues, or power struggles in your interactions and endeavors. You may encounter obstacles or resistance that challenge your ability to assert yourself or pursue your goals. It's essential to avoid power struggles and instead channel this intense energy into productive outlets.

27 Wednesday

Under the influence of the Scorpio Moon, emotions may run deep, and you may feel more attuned to the undercurrents of energy that shape your experiences. This lunar transit encourages you to recognize that true transformation often arises from facing and integrating the shadow aspects of your psyche. It's a time for emotional regeneration, shedding old layers of conditioning, and allowing yourself to be reborn from the ashes of past experiences.

28 Thursday

At 11:02 PM, Venus forms a challenging square aspect with Saturn, creating a sense of tension and restriction in matters of love, relationships, and finances. This aspect may bring about feelings of limitation, inhibition, or loneliness, as well as a sense of duty or responsibility weighing heavily on your heart. You may encounter obstacles or delays in your romantic or creative pursuits, as well as challenges in expressing affection or receiving love from others.

29 Friday

With Venus in Cancer transiting your third house, your communication style and intellectual pursuits become more nurturing and emotionally driven. You may find yourself focusing on practical ways to express your ideas with warmth and empathy. This period encourages you to embrace a gentle and compassionate approach to learning and communication, blending your natural curiosity with a desire for emotional connection and support.

30 Saturday

You may feel a strong desire for freedom, independence, and authenticity, as well as a thirst for knowledge and new perspectives. Use this time to expand your awareness, challenge your beliefs, and embrace the opportunities for growth and personal development that come your way. Embrace the spirit of Sagittarius Moon as you venture forth into the world with an open heart and a curious mind, ready to explore all that life has to offer.

31 Sunday

During this Full Moon, take time to reflect on your beliefs, aspirations, and goals. Celebrate your accomplishments and acknowledge the progress you have made since the New Moon. Release anything that no longer serves your highest good and set intentions for the future that align with your deepest desires and values. Embrace the adventurous spirit of Sagittarius and allow yourself to be guided by your intuition as you navigate the journey ahead.

JUNE

Mon	Tue	Wed	Thu	Fri	Sat	Sun
1	2	3	4	5	6	7
8	9	10	11	12	13	14
15	16	17	18	19	20	21
22	23	24	25	26	27	28
29	30					

New Moon

STRAWBERRY MOON

JUNE

1 Monday

Mercury transitions into the nurturing and sensitive sign of Cancer, infusing communication and thought processes with emotional depth and intuition. During this transit, you may find yourself more attuned to your feelings and those of others, seeking comfort and security in your interactions and decisions. Mercury in Cancer encourages you to trust your instincts and communicate with empathy as you navigate your daily conversations and exchanges.

2 Tuesday

Under the influence of the Sun sextile Saturn, you are encouraged to take practical steps toward your goals, leveraging your strengths and resources to build a solid foundation for success. It is a favorable time for planning, strategizing, and laying down the groundwork for future endeavors. You may also experience a greater sense of self-discipline and maturity, enabling you to overcome obstacles and persevere in the face of challenges.

3 Wednesday

Mercury sextiles the South Node at 7:39 AM. It creates a supportive aspect that facilitates the integration of past experiences and knowledge into your current endeavors. You may find yourself drawing upon insights gained from the past to navigate present challenges or communicate more effectively. This aspect encourages you to honor the wisdom of your journey and trust in the lessons learned while also remaining open to new perspectives and possibilities.

4 Thursday

Under the influence of Aquarius Moon, you may feel drawn to social causes, community involvement, and collective projects that aim to create positive change in the world. It is a time to celebrate diversity, embrace your unique quirks and talents, and contribute your insights and ideas to group endeavors. Embrace the innovative and visionary energy of Aquarius as you explore new possibilities, forge meaningful connections, and work towards a more harmonious society.

5 Friday

With Mars in Taurus transiting your first house, your drive and energy become more steadfast and determined. This period encourages you to pursue your goals with patience and persistence, focusing on long-term success. You may find yourself more grounded and practical in your approach to new challenges. It is a time to channel your energy into building a solid foundation for your ambitions, ensuring that your actions are sustainable and effective.

6 Saturday

It's a favorable period for self-reflection, meditation, and connecting with the divine within and around you. Allow yourself to surrender to the gentle currents of Piscean energy, trusting in the healing power of compassion, forgiveness, and unconditional love. By honoring your emotions and embracing the mysteries of the unseen realms, you can find solace, inspiration, and spiritual renewal amidst the ethereal beauty of the Piscean Moon's embrace.

7 Sunday

With Mercury in Cancer transiting your third house, your communication style and intellectual pursuits become more intuitive and nurturing. This period encourages you to engage in conversations and learning activities with a focus on empathy and emotional connection. You may find yourself more interested in exploring ideas and experiences that allow for deep and meaningful interactions. It is a time to channel your energy into enhancing your intellectual presence.

8 Monday

As the Moon wanes towards its New Moon phase, you are encouraged to embrace the energy of release and surrender. Letting go of what no longer serves your highest good allows space for new intentions to take root. Take this time to honor your journey, acknowledging both the achievements and lessons learned along the way. Trust in the natural cycles of growth and transformation, knowing that with each ending comes the potential for a fresh start.

9 Tuesday

At 4:33 AM, the Moon enters the fiery sign of Aries, infusing the atmosphere with energy, initiative, and a sense of spontaneity. You may find yourself feeling more assertive, courageous, and eager to take on new challenges. This lunar ingress ignites a desire for independence and individual expression, prompting you to pursue your goals with enthusiasm and determination. It's a time to trust your instincts, embrace your inner warrior, and fearlessly pursue your passions.

10 Wednesday

The Mercury square Saturn aspect exacts at 1:37 AM, suggesting a time when communication may feel constrained or challenged by limitations and obstacles. This aspect often brings about a sense of seriousness or heaviness in discussions, as well as potential delays or difficulties in conveying thoughts and ideas effectively. It's essential to approach communications with patience and a willingness to work through any setbacks that arise.

11 Thursday

The Moon's ingress into Taurus at 8:27 AM marks a shift in emotional focus and stability. Taurus, an earth sign ruled by Venus, brings a sense of groundedness, comfort, and sensuality to our emotions. During this transit, you may find yourself seeking security, stability, and pleasure in your surroundings. Emotions are likely to be steady and predictable, and there's a greater appreciation for the simple pleasures of life, such as good food, nature, and physical comforts.

12 Friday

Uranus square South Node indicates a confrontation with past patterns or behaviors that inhibit your growth. This aspect may bring upheaval or rebellion against established structures or limitations from your past. It encourages you to release outdated beliefs or attachments that no longer serve your evolution, freeing yourself from the constraints of history to embrace new possibilities for growth and liberation.

13 Saturday

The Moon moves into a curious and communicative Gemini, setting the stage for a day filled with mental stimulation, social connections, and variety. This lunar ingress enhances curiosity, adaptability, and the desire for intellectual engagement. It's a favorable time for networking, learning, and exchanging ideas. Embrace this energy by engaging in lively conversations, exploring new interests, and embracing the diversity of experiences that Gemini season offers.

14 Sunday

The New Moon occurring at 10:55 PM signifies the beginning of a new lunar cycle and a potent opportunity for fresh starts, intentions setting, and planting seeds for the future. This lunar phase marks a time of initiation, where the Moon and Sun align in the same zodiac sign, offering a powerful energy for manifestation and transformation. It's a moment to reflect on your goals, desires, and aspirations and to set intentions for what you wish to create or manifest in your life.

15 Monday

In the evening, at 6:52 PM, Venus forms a harmonious sextile with Uranus, introducing an element of excitement and innovation to relationships and creative endeavors. This aspect encourages spontaneity, originality, and a willingness to embrace change in matters of love and aesthetics. You may feel inspired to try new things, explore unconventional ideas, or connect with people who bring a sense of freshness into your life.

16 Tuesday

Venus forms a harmonious trine with Neptune, creating a celestial alignment that infuses relationships and emotional experiences with a dreamy and romantic energy. This aspect brings a sense of heightened sensitivity, empathy, and compassion to interactions and artistic endeavors. Under this influence, love and beauty are elevated to ethereal heights, and there's a desire to connect on a soulful level. It's a time when imagination flourishes and creative expression flows.

17 Wednesday

As the Moon enters Leo at 8:05 AM, you may notice a shift in your emotional landscape towards a more expressive and confident demeanor. This lunar ingress encourages you to embrace your creativity, seek attention, and express yourself with flair and passion. However, later in the day, Venus opposes Pluto at 4:38 PM, signaling potential challenges in your relationships and desires. You may encounter power struggles or intense emotions related to love, money, or values.

18 Thursday

A wave of cosmic energy ushers in a period of renewal, allowing you to break free from old routines and embrace exciting new possibilities. This fresh chapter promises growth and transformation, supported by the universe's alignment. As you open your heart to new experiences and connections, you will find yourself more inspired and motivated than ever before, ready to take on challenges with confidence and creativity.

19 Friday

With the influence of Virgo Moon, you're likely to feel more inclined towards organization and structure. It is an excellent time to take stock of your routines, tasks, and responsibilities and make necessary adjustments to ensure they align with your goals and priorities. You may find satisfaction in creating to-do lists, organizing your workspace or living environment, and implementing strategies that promote efficiency and effectiveness in your daily activities.

20 Saturday

Venus in Leo in the fourth house enhances your ability to manage family affairs with confidence and creativity. You may feel more driven to achieve domestic goals through bold and expressive efforts. It is a time to approach your home life with a confident and dynamic mindset. Your ability to create a warm and vibrant environment can lead to significant harmony and emotional well-being. The focus on creating an expressive home can enhance your family's security.

21 Sunday

The Moon reaches its First Quarter phase at 5:56 PM, marking a pivotal point in the lunar cycle. This phase encourages taking decisive action, overcoming challenges, and moving forward with intention and determination. It's a time for making adjustments, setting goals, and embracing the momentum of growth and progress in various areas of your life. Use this dynamic energy to assert yourself, tackle obstacles, and pursue your aspirations with confidence.

22 Monday

The stars illuminate a path of financial prosperity, presenting opportunities to increase your wealth and security through wise investments and strategic planning, building a solid foundation for future growth and stability that will support your aspirations and ensure a comfortable and secure future. This period of financial growth will also enable you to pursue your passions and dreams without the constraints of economic uncertainty.

23 Tuesday

The Sun's harmonious aspects with both the North Node and South Node provide a balanced approach to personal evolution. Embrace the opportunities presented to align with your soul's purpose while also honoring your past and integrating valuable lessons into your present path. This astrological configuration invites you to embrace growth, transformation, and the continuous journey of self-discovery with confidence and wisdom.

24 Wednesday

The Scorpio Moon energy amplifies passion, determination, and a desire for authenticity. You may feel more inclined to pursue your goals with unwavering focus, delve into research or investigative work, and seek profound connections in your relationships. This transit encourages you to embrace vulnerability, face fears or unresolved issues, and emerge more substantial and empowered from emotional challenges.

25 Thursday

Later in the day, at 6:38 PM, the Sun squares Neptune, creating a dynamic tension between your ego and the realm of dreams, illusions, and spirituality. This aspect can bring about confusion, uncertainty, or a sense of disillusionment, especially if there are discrepancies between reality and idealized visions. You may need to exercise caution in decision-making, as there could be tendencies towards self-deception or encountering deceptive influences from others.

26 Friday

Under the influence of the Sagittarius Moon, you may feel a strong desire for freedom, exploration, and learning. It is a great time to engage in activities that stimulate your mind, such as travel, higher education, philosophical discussions, or pursuing new interests and hobbies. You may also feel drawn to expand your social circle, connect with people from diverse backgrounds, and engage in meaningful conversations that broaden your perspective.

27 Saturday

The Sun in Cancer in the third house enhances your ability to engage with others and absorb new information quickly. You're likely to be more pleasant and eager to share your ideas, making this an excellent time for networking and building relationships. This influence can bring about a period of intellectual growth as you explore new subjects and exchange ideas with others. By staying curious and communicative, you can make the most of opportunities for learning.

28 Sunday

The Mars-Jupiter sextile encourages you to channel your energy into productive endeavors, embrace challenges with courage, and believe in your abilities to overcome obstacles. It's a favorable time for initiating new projects, expanding your horizons, and pushing beyond your comfort zone. You may also experience a boost in motivation, vitality, and a sense of purpose as you strive towards your aspirations.

JULY

Mon	Tue	Wed	Thu	Fri	Sat	Sun
		1	2	3	4	5
6	7	8	9	10	11	12
13	14	15	16	17	18	19
20	21	22	23	24	25	26
27	28	29	30	31		

NEW MOON

Buck Moon

_____

_____

_____

_____

_____

_____

_____

_____

_____

_____

_____

_____

_____

_____

_____

_____

_____

_____

30 Monday

The astrological landscape takes a turn at 1:35 PM when Mercury, the planet of communication and intellect, turns retrograde. Mercury retrograde periods are known for potential communication glitches, misunderstandings, delays, and revisiting past issues. During this time, it's essential to double-check information, be patient with communication delays, and avoid making significant decisions or signing contracts without careful consideration.

31 Tuesday

At 2:07 AM, Jupiter transitions into the bold and confident sign of Leo. This ingress brings a surge of optimism, creativity, and a desire for self-expression. Jupiter in Leo encourages you to embrace your unique talents, pursue your passions with enthusiasm, and seek opportunities that allow you to shine brightly. This planetary shift enhances your confidence, expands your horizons, and fosters a spirit of generosity and leadership.

1 Wednesday

The Aquarius Moon encourages experimentation, spontaneity, and thinking outside the box. Embrace opportunities to break free from limitations, explore unconventional approaches, and embrace the power of collective wisdom and collaboration. Allow yourself to be open to new experiences, embrace your authenticity, and contribute your unique insights and talents to collective endeavors during this lunar transit.

2 Thursday

With the Sun in Cancer transiting your third house, your focus is on communication, learning, and local connections. This period encourages you to embrace your curiosity and engage in stimulating conversations. You may feel more inclined to share your knowledge and connect with your community. Use this time to enhance your communication skills and expand your intellectual horizons. A versatile approach to learning helps you gain valuable insights.

JULY

3 Friday

Cosmic energies foster a sense of community and belonging, drawing you towards groups and organizations that share your values and interests, creating opportunities for meaningful connections and collaborative efforts that bring joy and fulfillment. As you engage with these communities, you will find that they provide valuable support and inspiration, helping you achieve your goals and enrich your life.

4 Saturday

Under the influence of the Pisces Moon, you may experience heightened empathy, compassion, and a desire for emotional connection. It is a favorable time for artistic expression, spiritual practices, and engaging in activities that nourish your soul and foster a sense of inner peace. Allow yourself to tap into your imagination, intuition, and emotional sensitivity to gain deeper insights into your emotions and the world around you.

5 Sunday

The Mars trine Pluto aspect invites you to explore the depths of your psyche, confront fears or insecurities, and tap into your inner reservoir of strength and resilience. This aspect can bring a sense of empowerment, self-discovery, and the courage to break through barriers that have been holding you back. It encourages you to embrace authenticity, face challenges with confidence, and take decisive action toward creating the life you desire.

JULY

6 Monday

The Moon transitions into assertive Aries at 11:07 AM, bringing a wave of dynamic and courageous energy. The Aries Moon encourages you to embrace action, assertiveness, and a pioneering spirit. You may feel more confident, motivated, and ready to take initiative in pursuing your goals and expressing your individuality. This lunar ingress ignites a desire for independence, adventure, and a willingness to take risks in pursuit of personal fulfillment.

7 Tuesday

With Neptune turning retrograde, a subtle yet introspective energy permeates the day. Neptune, the planet of dreams, illusions, and spirituality, begins its retrograde journey, prompting you to delve into your subconscious mind, explore hidden truths, and reassess your spiritual beliefs and practices. This retrograde period invites you to reflect on illusions or escapisms that may be clouding your perception and encourages a deeper connection with your inner wisdom.

8 Wednesday

Under the influence of the Taurus Moon, you may feel inclined to indulge in self-care, enjoy delicious meals, or create a cozy and harmonious environment at home. This lunar ingress promotes a sense of calmness, patience, and appreciation for life's simple pleasures. It's a favorable time for financial planning, building stability, and tending to practical matters with a steady and systematic approach. Embrace this period as an opportunity to nurture your body, mind, and spirit.

9 Thursday

When Venus transitions into Virgo at 1:25 PM, a shift towards practicality, attention to detail, and a focus on service and improvement takes place. The Virgo ingress of Venus encourages you to approach relationships, aesthetics, and pleasures with a discerning eye and a desire for perfection. Use this time to pay attention to the finer details, enhance your organization skills, and seek beauty in simplicity and functionality.

10 Friday

Under the influence of the Gemini Moon, you may find yourself more friendly, intellectually curious, and eager to explore various interests and perspectives. It's a favorable time for networking, brainstorming, and expanding your knowledge base through conversations and interactions with others. Embrace the energy of curiosity, flexibility, and open-mindedness as you navigate social dynamics and seek opportunities for mental stimulation and growth.

11 Saturday

Cosmic energies support the formation of new partnerships and alliances, both personal and professional, that have the potential to bring mutual benefit and success, fostering collaboration and synergy that propel you toward your goals. As you build these connections, you will find that they provide valuable support and encouragement, making your journey towards achievement more enjoyable and fulfilling.

12 Sunday

The Cancer Moon encourages introspection, self-care, and creating a sense of sanctuary in your surroundings. It is a time to prioritize comfort, rest, and activities that replenish your soul. Embrace rituals that promote emotional healing, such as journaling, meditation, or spending quiet time in nature. Use this period to recharge your emotional batteries and create a harmonious balance between inner peace and external responsibilities.

13 Monday

When Venus forms a square aspect with Uranus at 10:26 AM, electrifying and unpredictable energy permeates the day, bringing potential surprises, changes, and disruptions in matters of love, relationships, and finances. This aspect may trigger sudden shifts, unexpected events, or a desire for freedom and independence in your interactions and values. It's a time to remain adaptable and open-minded, embracing the opportunities for growth and excitement that may arise.

14 Tuesday

The Moon transitions into vibrant and expressive Leo, infusing the atmosphere with creativity, passion, and a desire for recognition and self-expression. The Leo Moon encourages you to embrace your uniqueness, showcase your talents, and express yourself authentically. This lunar ingress sparks enthusiasm, confidence, and a need for creative outlets and playful self-expression. Use this period to embrace your inner spark and share your gifts with the world.

15 Wednesday

When Uranus forms a sextile aspect with Neptune at 4:35 PM, harmonious and creative energy permeates the day, blending innovation with spirituality and imagination. This planetary alignment brings opportunities for inspiration, intuitive insights, and a deeper connection to higher consciousness. It's a favorable time to tap into your creativity, trust your intuition, and explore innovative ideas that bridge the gap between the material and spiritual realms.

16 Thursday

Overall, the Moon's ingress into Virgo invites you to embrace a practical and organized approach to life. Take advantage of this period to attend to details, enhance productivity, and create a harmonious and efficient environment that supports your goals and well-being. Trust in your ability to manage tasks effectively, prioritize self-care, and make practical improvements that contribute to your overall success and fulfillment.

17 Friday

With Mars in Gemini transiting your second house, your approach to finances and material possessions becomes more dynamic and resourceful. This period encourages you to focus on generating income and managing your assets through diverse strategies. You may find yourself more willing to take calculated risks and explore multiple streams of revenue. It is a time to channel your energy into building financial stability with innovative and adaptable methods.

18 Saturday

When Uranus forms a trine aspect with Pluto at 12:43 AM, a powerful and transformative energy infuses the cosmic landscape, heralding a period of profound change, innovation, and regeneration. This harmonious alignment between the revolutionary Uranus and the regenerative Pluto signifies a time of profound shifts, breakthroughs, and empowerment on both personal and collective levels. It's a cosmic invitation to embrace change and evolution.

19 Sunday

At 2:10 PM, Mars forms a sextile aspect with Saturn, bringing a blend of discipline, determination, and strategic action to the forefront. This planetary alignment encourages you to take structured and methodical steps toward your goals, utilizing perseverance, patience, and practicality. The Mars-Saturn sextile aspect empowers you to make steady progress, overcome obstacles, and achieve long-term success through focused effort and disciplined action.

20 Monday

Jupiter opposes Pluto, creating a dynamic tension between expansion and transformation. This aspect challenges you to confront power dynamics, hidden truths, and areas of growth and evolution in your life. It may bring up issues related to control, authority, or the need for profound transformation. Embrace the transformative energy of the Jupiter-Pluto opposition as an opportunity to release old patterns and tap into your power to create positive change.

21 Tuesday

When the Moon reaches its First Quarter phase at 7:06 AM, a dynamic energy of initiative, action, and growth permeates the day, urging you to take decisive steps toward your goals and intentions set during the New Moon. This lunar phase marks a crucial point in the lunar cycle, encouraging you to assess your progress, make necessary adjustments, and push forward with determination and focus. Use this time to evaluate your goals and plans and take proactive steps.

22 Wednesday

The Sun's ingress into Leo encourages you to embrace creativity, self-expression, and a sense of purpose in your endeavors. It is a favorable time for pursuing artistic projects, engaging in activities that bring you joy, and expressing yourself authentically. Allow yourself to explore new avenues of creativity, take bold initiatives, and embrace the excitement. Let your passion guide you, and don't be afraid to take calculated risks and showcase your talents with confidence.

23 Thursday

Overall, today's astrological influences highlight a shift towards more precise communication and a sense of adventure and exploration. Embrace the clarity brought by Mercury turning direct, use the Sagittarius Moon's energy to expand your horizons and embrace new experiences, and approach life with optimism, curiosity, and a willingness to learn and grow. Trust in the journey ahead and remain open to the opportunities that come your way.

24 Friday

Overall, the Mercury-Venus sextile invites you to embrace harmonious communication, express your feelings authentically, and appreciate the beauty and creativity around you. Use this time to nurture your relationships, express love and gratitude, and engage in activities that uplift your spirit and inspire creativity. Trust in the power of heartfelt communication and let your words and actions reflect your genuine feelings and intentions.

25 Saturday

The Neptune-Pluto sextile encourages you to embrace your intuition, trust your inner guidance, and connect with the more profound mysteries of existence. Use this cosmic alignment to engage in practices such as meditation, journaling, or spiritual exploration, allowing you to access higher realms of consciousness and gain clarity on your life's purpose and spiritual journey. Allow the gentle flow of Neptune's intuitive energy and Pluto's transformative power to guide you.

26 Sunday

At 9:02 PM, the North Node shifts into Aquarius, while the South Node enters Leo simultaneously. This nodal axis transition emphasizes themes of collective growth, innovation, and balancing individuality with collaboration. The North Node in Aquarius encourages you to embrace progressive ideas, contribute to community initiatives, and explore unconventional paths forward. Meanwhile, the South Node in Leo invites you to release ego-driven patterns.

27 Monday

The Sun forms a harmonious trine aspect with Neptune, infusing the atmosphere with a dreamy, intuitive, and spiritually uplifting energy. This alignment encourages you to tap into your imagination, connect with your intuition, and explore your spiritual or creative pursuits with inspiration and sensitivity. Use this cosmic synergy to engage in practices such as meditation, visualization, or artistic expression that nourish your soul and deepen your connection with the divine.

28 Tuesday

Under the influence of the Aquarius Moon, you may feel more inclined towards unconventional thinking, progressive ideas, and a desire to contribute to collective efforts that promote social justice, equality, and freedom. This lunar ingress invites you to explore new perspectives, challenge the status quo, and collaborate with others to create meaningful impact and positive change. Embrace the energy of innovation and forward-thinking as you navigate opportunities for growth.

29 Wednesday

When Venus forms a square aspect with Mars at 3:09 AM, a dynamic and potentially challenging energy arises in matters related to love, relationships, and desires. This aspect may bring about tension, conflicts of interest, or power struggles between the feminine and masculine energies within and in relationships. It's essential to navigate this influence with patience, understanding, and a willingness to find balance and compromise.

30 Thursday

The Sun in Leo in the fourth house enhances your ability to create a joyful and harmonious home environment. You're likely to be more focused on your family's well-being and more willing to invest in your domestic life. This influence can bring about a period of positive change in your home as you prioritize your family's happiness and make improvements that reflect your values. By staying true to your sense of style, you can create a more fulfilling and loving home life.

AUGUST

Mon	Tue	Wed	Thu	Fri	Sat	Sun
					1	2
3	4	5	6	7	8	9
10	11	12	13	14	15	16
17	18	19	20	21	22	23
24	25	26	27	28	29	30
31						

New Moon

STURGEON MOON

31 Friday

When the Moon transitions into Pisces at 8:14 AM, a dreamy, imaginative, and sensitive energy permeates the cosmic atmosphere, inviting you to delve into the realms of intuition, creativity, and emotional depth. The Pisces Moon encourages compassion, empathy, and a deep connection with your inner world and the unseen aspects of life. Allow yourself to surrender to the flow of emotions and tap into the intuitive wisdom that Pisces brings.

1 Saturday

With Venus in Virgo transiting your fifth house, your approach to creativity, romance, and recreation becomes more refined and detail-oriented. You may find yourself focusing on ways to develop your talents and enjoy your leisure activities with precision and practicality. This period encourages you to embrace a thoughtful and meticulous approach to creative expression, blending your natural enthusiasm with a desire for order and improvement.

2 Sunday

Under the influence of the Aries Moon, you may feel a strong urge to assert yourself, tackle challenges head-on, and embrace new beginnings with confidence. This lunar ingress invites you to tap into your inner warrior spirit, overcome obstacles, and channel your energy into productive and action-oriented pursuits. Allow the fiery energy of Aries to fuel your passion and inspire you to take decisive action in pursuit of your dreams.

3 Monday

The universe is showering you with the energy of resilience and perseverance, reminding you of your inner strength and ability to overcome challenges. This period calls for determination and grit as you navigate obstacles and pursue your goals with unwavering resolve. The celestial forces are on your side, providing the support and encouragement needed to rise above difficulties and achieve success through sheer tenacity.

4 Tuesday

Today's lunar ingress into Taurus invites you to embrace a sense of groundedness, security, and appreciation for life's blessings. Take time to slow down, connect with nature, and enjoy moments of relaxation and indulgence. Trust in the steady and nurturing energy of the Taurus Moon to support you in creating a sense of stability, abundance, and harmony in your life. Embrace the pleasures of the present moment and cultivate a mindset of gratitude and abundance.

5 Wednesday

The Moon reaches its Last Quarter phase at 10:22 PM, marking a time of reflection, release, and completion in the lunar cycle. This phase occurs when the Moon is halfway between the Full Moon and the New Moon, symbolizing a turning point where energies begin to wane. It's a favorable period for evaluating progress, letting go of what no longer serves you, and preparing for new beginnings. Embrace this phase as an opportunity to make adjustments.

6 Thursday

Later in the day, at 10:44 PM, the Sun forms a supportive trine aspect with Saturn, bringing a sense of stability, discipline, and practicality to the forefront. This aspect encourages you to take a structured and responsible approach to your goals, commitments, and long-term plans. Use the Sun trine Saturn aspect to establish a solid foundation, set realistic goals, and implement strategies that promote long-lasting success and fulfillment.

7 Friday

Use this time to express your thoughts and ideas, engage in brainstorming sessions, and seek out opportunities for growth. The Gemini Moon supports activities such as studying, writing, networking, and engaging in light-hearted social gatherings that promote lively discussions and exchanges of information. Embrace the dynamic energy of the Gemini Moon to expand your knowledge and connect with like-minded individuals who inspire your intellectual curiosity.

8 Saturday

With the Sun in Leo transiting your fourth house, your focus is on home, family, and emotional foundations. This period encourages you to create a warm and welcoming environment within your domestic sphere. You may feel more inclined to take pride in your home and strengthen your family bonds. Use this time to enhance your living space and ensure that it reflects your personality. A confident approach to domestic matters helps you create a supportive home life.

9 Sunday

Under the influence of the Cancer Moon, you may feel more attuned to your emotions, seeking comfort and support from loved ones and familiar environments. This lunar ingress invites you to nurture yourself and others, express empathy and compassion, and create a harmonious atmosphere that fosters emotional healing and connection. Use this time to engage in stimulating activities that soothe your soul and deepen your bonds with those you hold dear.

10 Monday

Venus opposes Neptune, creating a dynamic tension between love, dreams, and illusions. This aspect may bring about romantic idealism, inspiration, or moments of confusion in relationships. It's essential to navigate this aspect with clarity and discernment, being mindful of unrealistic expectations or romantic fantasies that may cloud your judgment. Use this time to seek clarity, communicate openly, and ensure that your relationships are built on a foundation of honesty.

11 Tuesday

Mercury forms a harmonious trine aspect with Neptune at 11:40 PM, enhancing intuition, creativity, and spiritual insights in communication and mental pursuits. This aspect encourages empathy, compassion, and imaginative thinking, making it an ideal time for artistic expression, spiritual conversations, and intuitive insights. Trust your intuition and allow your creativity to flow freely, tapping into the deeper realms of consciousness for inspiration and clarity.

12 Wednesday

The New Moon at 1:37 PM marks a potent time for new beginnings, fresh starts, and setting intentions for the lunar cycle ahead. This lunar phase invites you to plant seeds of intention, visualize your goals, and initiate projects or changes that align with your deepest desires and aspirations. Embrace the energy of renewal and transformation, allowing yourself to let go of the old and embrace the new with optimism and excitement.

13 Thursday

Mercury forms a harmonious sextile aspect with Venus, enhancing communication, social interactions, and harmonious connections. This aspect encourages pleasant conversations, diplomatic exchanges, and a focus on cooperation and understanding in relationships. Use this favorable energy to express appreciation, resolve conflicts amicably, and engage in heartfelt conversations with loved ones. Tap into the harmonious flow of communication.

14 Friday

Embrace today's astrological influences to harness your inner strength, embrace transformational opportunities, and take decisive action toward your goals. Trust in your ability to navigate challenges, stay focused on your priorities, and tap into your inner resilience and determination for success. Allow yourself to explore your passions, cultivate a sense of purpose, and move forward with courage and determination on your path to personal growth.

15 Saturday

Embrace the optimistic energy of the Mercury-Jupiter conjunction to pursue intellectual growth, share ideas with confidence, and engage in positive communication. Utilize the Moon's ingress into Libra to foster harmonious relationships, promote cooperation, and create a peaceful and balanced atmosphere in your interactions. Trust in your ability to communicate effectively, seek common ground, and foster understanding as you navigate the day's energies.

16 Sunday

Mercury in Leo in the fourth house enhances your ability to manage family communications with creativity and confidence. You may feel more driven to achieve household goals through inventive and resourceful efforts. Embrace this opportunity to refine your family dynamics, creating a lively and harmonious household. Your leadership skills can help resolve domestic issues effectively, fostering a supportive and cooperative atmosphere at home.

17 Monday

Mercury forms a supportive trine aspect with Saturn, fostering disciplined thinking, strategic planning, and effective communication. This aspect encourages practicality, organization, and attention to detail in your thoughts and interactions. Use this time to focus on long-term goals, implement structured approaches, and communicate with clarity and authority. Embrace the steady and methodical energy of Mercury trine Saturn to achieve tangible results.

18 Tuesday

With Venus in Libra transiting your sixth house, your approach to work, health, and daily routines becomes more balanced and harmonious. You may find yourself focusing on ways to improve your productivity and well-being with grace and diplomacy. This period encourages you to embrace a thoughtful and diplomatic approach to your daily tasks, blending your natural energy with a desire for balance and social harmony.

19 Wednesday

Utilize the dynamic energy of the First Quarter Moon to set priorities, prioritize tasks, and maintain a sense of momentum in pursuing your dreams and ambitions. Trust in your abilities, stay adaptable to change, and keep your vision in sight as you navigate the opportunities and challenges that come your way during this phase of the lunar cycle. Embrace the energy of growth and transformation, allowing yourself to evolve and expand in alignment with your goals.

20 Thursday

Embrace the adventurous spirit of the Sagittarius Moon to embark on new journeys, whether they are literal travels or journeys of the mind and soul. Explore different cultures, philosophies, or belief systems, and embrace diversity in thought and experience. Allow yourself to step out of your comfort zone and embrace the unknown with a sense of excitement and openness. Trust in the transformative power of exploration and discovery as you expand your horizons.

21 Friday

When Venus opposes Saturn at 8:42 AM, a sense of tension and restriction may arise in matters related to love, relationships, and finances. This aspect can bring about challenges in expressing affection, experiencing joy, or achieving harmony in partnerships. It's essential to be patient, realistic, and responsible in your interactions and commitments during this time. Embrace the lessons that the Venus-Saturn opposition brings, such as the need for boundaries or commitment.

22 Saturday

The Sun opposes the North Node and conjuncts the South Node simultaneously, highlighting a period of karmic reflection, letting go of old patterns, and aligning with your life's purpose. The Sun opposing the North Node may bring about tensions between personal desires and spiritual growth, urging you to find a balance between self-expression and collective evolution. Meanwhile, the Sun conjunct the South Node calls for releasing past habits, beliefs, and behaviors.

23 Sunday

Mars in Cancer in the third house enhances your ability to communicate with empathy and emotional depth. You may feel more driven to achieve intellectual goals through emotionally guided efforts. It is a time to approach your studies and interactions with a nurturing and intuitive mindset, allowing your emotional insight to lead to deeper understanding. Embrace this opportunity to strengthen your communication skills, creating connections that are heartfelt and engaging.

24 Monday

The Sun in Virgo in the fifth house enhances your ability to approach creative projects with dedication and precision. You're likely to be more disciplined in pursuing your passions, making it an excellent time to develop your talents. This influence can bring about a period of artistic growth as you focus on improving your skills and creating meaningful works. By embracing a practical approach to self-expression, you can achieve tremendous success in your creative pursuits.

25 Tuesday

Mercury transitions into Virgo, bringing a focus on practicality, organization, and analytical thinking. This Mercury ingress encourages you to pay attention to details, improve efficiency, and approach tasks with precision and clarity. Use this time to implement effective communication strategies, prioritize tasks, and refine your plans for greater productivity and success. Embrace the Virgo Mercury's energy to enhance your mental clarity and problem-solving abilities.

26 Wednesday

Cosmic energies enhance your sense of adventure and curiosity, inviting you to explore new territories and embrace novel experiences. Whether through travel, learning new skills, or stepping out of your comfort zone, this is a time to broaden your horizons and discover the richness of life. The universe encourages you to embark on exciting journeys that expand your perspective and bring a sense of exhilaration and fulfillment.

27 Thursday

Embrace the synergy between the Sun-Mercury conjunction and the Moon in Pisces to enhance both your logical thinking and emotional depth. Utilize your heightened communication skills to express empathy, listen actively to others, and bridge understanding in your interactions. Trust your intuition and allow yourself to be guided by your inner wisdom as you navigate this harmonious blend of intellectual clarity and emotional sensitivity.

28 Friday

At 3:24 AM, Mercury forms a challenging square aspect with Uranus, creating a dynamic and potentially disruptive energy in communication, thinking processes, and information exchange. This aspect may bring sudden insights, unexpected news, or a need for mental flexibility and adaptability. Stay open-minded, think outside the box, and be prepared for surprises or changes in plans that require quick thinking and innovative solutions.

29 Saturday

As the Moon enters Aries, you may feel a surge of energy and a desire to initiate change or tackle challenges head-on. Use this assertive and pioneering energy to overcome obstacles, break through limitations, and make progress toward your aspirations. Stay focused on your goals, stay resilient in the face of challenges, and harness the courage of the Aries Moon to move forward with confidence and determination. Embrace the fiery spirit of Aries to ignite your passions.

30 Sunday

Mercury in Virgo in the fifth house enhances your ability to channel your creative energies into detailed and precise endeavors. You may feel more driven to achieve artistic and romantic goals through meticulous and well-organized efforts. Embrace this opportunity to refine your creative and romantic life, creating experiences that are both stimulating and fulfilling. Your practical approach can attract romantic interests and inspire artistic collaborations.

SEPTEMBER

Mon	Tue	Wed	Thu	Fri	Sat	Sun
	1	2	3	4	5	6
7	8	9	10	11	12	13
14	15	16	17	18	19	20
21	22	23	24	25	26	27
28	29	30				

NEW MOON

CORN/HARVEST MOON

31 Monday

The Jupiter trine Saturn aspect brings a sense of balance, harmony, and stability to your endeavors, making it an ideal time to consolidate efforts, set realistic goals, and implement long-term strategies for success. This cosmic alignment encourages you to blend optimism with practicality, allowing you to make sound decisions and build a solid foundation for future growth. Embrace the opportunities that arise during this period to expand your horizons.

1 Tuesday

Embrace the practical and nurturing energy of the Taurus Moon to create a sense of stability and comfort. Navigate challenges with patience and strategic thinking during the Mars-Saturn square, and utilize the clarity and assertiveness of the Mercury-Mars sextile to communicate effectively and pursue your objectives with confidence. Trust in your abilities to overcome obstacles, stay resilient, and make progress toward your goals during this dynamic astrological period.

2 Wednesday

With the Sun in Virgo transiting your fifth house, your focus is on creativity, romance, and self-expression. This period encourages you to bring a meticulous and practical approach to your creative endeavors. You may feel more inclined to refine your skills and pay attention to the details in your work. Use this time to engage in activities that bring joy and allow you to express your individuality. A careful approach to creativity will help you produce high-quality work.

3 Thursday

Embrace the lively and communicative energy of the Gemini Moon to foster connections, express yourself creatively, and embrace a diversity of perspectives. Stay open-minded, curious, and adaptable as you navigate this dynamic and intellectually stimulating lunar transit. Trust in your ability to communicate effectively, learn from others, and enjoy the richness of new experiences during this time. Allow the Gemini Moon to inspire curiosity and creativity.

4 Friday

As the Moon enters its Last Quarter, you may feel an urgency to wrap up loose ends and make decisions that align with your long-term goals. Embrace this phase as an opportunity to evaluate your achievements, learn from challenges, and refine your plans for the future. Trust in your intuition and wisdom as you navigate this transitional period and prepare for the next phase of growth and transformation. Use the reflective energy of the Last Quarter Moon to gain clarity.

5 Saturday

The Moon's ingress into Cancer at 10:30 AM invites you to prioritize emotional well-being, self-nurturing, and creating a supportive home environment. Take time to listen to your inner voice, honor your feelings, and nurture your soul through activities that bring you comfort and emotional fulfillment. Use the Cancer Moon's nurturing energy to deepen your connections with loved ones, foster a sense of belonging, and create a harmonious and loving atmosphere.

6 Sunday

The stars are aligning to foster a sense of gratitude and contentment, reminding you to appreciate the blessings and joys in your life. This period is perfect for practicing mindfulness, savoring the present moment, and expressing thanks for the abundance you have. The cosmic energy helps you to cultivate a positive outlook and a heart filled with gratitude, which attracts even more blessings and enhances your overall sense of happiness and fulfillment.

7 Monday

Embrace the vibrant and expressive energy of the Moon's ingress into Leo at 12:49 PM. This lunar transit invites you to shine brightly, embrace your passions, and express yourself with confidence and enthusiasm. Allow your creativity to flourish, share your unique gifts with others, and bask in the sense of pride and satisfaction that comes with embracing your true self. Use the Leo Moon's energy to inspire others, pursue your dreams, and enjoy the journey of self-discovery.

8 Tuesday

The universe is aligning to bring a sense of purpose and direction to your career, encouraging you to pursue work that aligns with your values and passions. This period is perfect for setting career goals, seeking opportunities that resonate with your purpose, and taking steps to advance your professional path. The celestial energies support your career journey, guiding you toward fulfilling and meaningful work that brings satisfaction and success.

9 Wednesday

Embrace the practical and detail-oriented energy of the Moon's ingress into Virgo at 3:35 PM. This lunar transit invites you to focus on productivity, organization, and efficiency in your daily life. Take advantage of this time to tackle tasks methodically, streamline your routines, and pay attention to the details that contribute to your overall success and well-being. Use the Virgo Moon's analytical energy to make practical improvements and create a sense of order and balance.

10 Thursday

The alignment of Venus trine the North Node and sextile the South Node at 2:07 AM signifies a harmonious connection between relationships, love, and karmic growth. This aspect encourages you to embrace opportunities for meaningful connections, partnerships, and positive interactions that align with your soul's path and evolution. Use this time to nurture supportive relationships, express love and appreciation, and align your actions with your higher purpose.

11 Friday

As the Moon enters Libra, you may feel a heightened awareness of beauty, aesthetics, and the importance of creating a harmonious environment. Embrace this energy by surrounding yourself with beauty, engaging in artistic activities, and appreciating the elegance in your surroundings. Use the Libra Moon's influence to enhance your sense of style, promote peace in your relationships, and seek out moments of grace and refinement.

12 Saturday

The Mercury trine Pluto aspect at 11:58 AM signifies a time of deep insights, intense focus, and profound communication. This aspect empowers you to delve into the depths of your mind, uncover hidden truths, and express your thoughts with clarity and conviction. Use this alignment to engage in meaningful conversations, research projects, and transformative discussions that can lead to powerful changes and personal growth.

13 Sunday

The trine between Mercury and Uranus enhances your ability to grasp complex concepts quickly, adapt to changing circumstances, and express your ideas in unique and exciting ways. This aspect favors brainstorming sessions, technological advancements, and out-of-the-box thinking. Embrace the electric energy of Mercury trine Uranus to break free from mental limitations, embrace your eccentricities, and share your vision for the future.

14 Monday

The Black Moon's ingress into Capricorn at 1:37 PM adds a sense of seriousness, discipline, and a desire for long-term stability. This placement encourages you to take practical steps toward your goals, establish firm boundaries, and seek a sense of authority or responsibility in your endeavors. Embrace this energy by creating a structured plan of action, prioritizing tasks, and committing to achieving your objectives with determination and perseverance.

15 Tuesday

The Neptune sextile Pluto aspect at 10:10 PM offers a harmonious blend of spirituality, intuition, and transformational energy. This aspect supports deep healing, spiritual insights, and a sense of compassion and empathy towards others. Use this alignment to tap into your intuition, connect with higher realms of consciousness, and engage in soulful practices that enhance your spiritual journey. Embrace this time to explore your spiritual beliefs.

16 Wednesday

Overall, today's astrological influence of the Moon in Sagittarius encourages you to embrace a mindset of adventure, curiosity, and possibility. Allow yourself to be guided by your intuition and inner wisdom as you navigate new opportunities and experiences. Trust in your ability to adapt, learn, and grow, knowing that each step you take toward the unknown brings valuable lessons and opportunities for personal expansion.

17 Thursday

With Venus in Scorpio transiting your seventh house, your relationships and partnerships take on a deeper, more intense dynamic. This period encourages you to explore the hidden depths of your connections, seeking out truth and authenticity. You may find yourself drawn to partners who offer profound emotional experiences, challenging you to grow. It is a time to embrace vulnerability and deepen your bonds through mutual trust and understanding.

18 Friday

Today's astrological influences highlight the need for patience, practicality, and strategic action. Navigate the Mercury-Saturn opposition with a grounded mindset, seeking practical solutions and staying resilient in the face of challenges. Embrace the energy of the First Quarter Moon to take the initiative, make adjustments where needed, and move forward with confidence toward your goals. Trust in your abilities to overcome obstacles and stay focused on your path.

19 Saturday

Today's astrological influence of the Moon in Capricorn inspires you to embrace a holistic approach to success, combining ambition with practicality, resilience with strategic planning, and dedication with integrity. Stay grounded in your values, trust in your inner strength, and keep your eyes on the prize as you chart your course toward achievement and fulfillment. It is a time to align your actions with your vision and take deliberate steps toward your goals.

20 Sunday

Celestial energies are urging you to cultivate a sense of gratitude and appreciation for the blessings in your life, encouraging you to acknowledge and celebrate the good things around you. It is a time for practicing gratitude daily, expressing thanks to others, and recognizing the abundance in your life. The universe supports your efforts to cultivate gratitude, guiding you toward a mindset of positivity and appreciation that attracts even more blessings.

21 Monday

The Mercury-Jupiter sextile encourages open-mindedness, curiosity, and a thirst for knowledge. It's a favorable time for learning, teaching, and exchanging ideas with others who inspire you intellectually. Use this cosmic alignment to broaden your horizons, explore new interests, and approach challenges with a sense of optimism and confidence. Trust in the power of positive thinking and expansive vision as you navigate this harmonious alignment.

22 Tuesday

The convergence of the September Equinox and the Sun's ingress into Libra invites you to explore themes of balance, fairness, and collaboration in various aspects of your life. It's a time to reassess your priorities, realign with your values, and seek harmony within yourself and with the world around you. Embrace the energies of balance and partnership as guiding principles on your journey of personal growth and fulfillment.

23 Wednesday

Under the influence of the Pisces Moon, you may find yourself more attuned to the emotions of others, drawn to artistic expression, and seeking moments of quiet introspection. This lunar ingress invites you to embrace your intuitive side, trust your inner guidance, and explore the depths of your subconscious mind for inspiration and insight. It's a time to honor your feelings, nurture your creative spirit, and connect with the mystical dimensions of existence.

24 Thursday

Mercury in Libra in the sixth house enhances your ability to manage your work and health with balance and fairness. You may feel more driven to achieve professional and personal goals through harmonious and well-organized efforts. Embrace this opportunity to transform your daily habits, creating a lifestyle that is both productive and fulfilling. Your diplomatic skills can lead to increased cooperation and effectiveness in your work environment.

25 Friday

Under the influence of the Sun-Neptune opposition, you may experience a heightened sensitivity, intuitive insights, and a stronger connection to the spiritual realms. However, it's essential to remain grounded and discerning, as this aspect can also blur boundaries and lead to confusion or escapism if not approached with awareness. Use this energy to delve into your creative pursuits, explore your dreams and aspirations, and tap into the deeper layers of your subconscious mind.

26 Saturday

The Moon gracefully transitions into Aries at 6:23 AM, infusing the cosmic landscape with energies of courage, initiative, and vitality. The Aries Moon's influence encourages you to take bold action, assert your individuality, and pursue your passions with enthusiasm and determination. This lunar ingress ignites a spark of inspiration, motivating you to step into new beginnings and embrace opportunities for personal growth and self-expression.

27 Sunday

As Mars ignites Leo's fiery energy, you're encouraged to tap into your creativity, passion, and inner drive to pursue what sets your soul on fire. Use this cosmic alignment to channel your energy into creative projects, leadership roles, and activities that bring you joy and fulfillment. Leverage the confidence and assertiveness of Mars in Leo to express yourself boldly, take initiative, and make a positive impact in your personal and professional endeavors.

October

Mon	Tue	Wed	Thu	Fri	Sat	Sun
			1	2	3	4
5	6	7	8	9	10	11
12	13	14	15	16	17	18
19	20	21	22	23	24	25
26	27	28	29	30	31	

NEW MOON

HUNTERS MOON

28 Monday

Under the influence of the Taurus Moon, you're encouraged to savor the present moment, indulge in sensory experiences, and cultivate a sense of gratitude for the abundance in your life. This lunar phase supports activities that bring you comfort, pleasure, and a sense of security, whether through enjoying good food, spending time in nature, or engaging in creative pursuits. Embrace the tranquility of Taurus energy, find joy in simple pleasures, and take time to nurture your body and soul.

29 Tuesday

Mercury forms a supportive sextile with the South Node at 6:03 PM, offering opportunities for reflection, integration, and releasing old patterns or beliefs that no longer serve your highest good. This aspect encourages you to draw upon past experiences, wisdom, and insights to inform your present decisions and communication style. It's a time to honor your journey, acknowledge lessons learned, and apply your knowledge in practical ways.

30 Wednesday

The Mercury's ingress into Scorpio and the Moon's shift into Gemini create a dynamic blend of deep introspection and mental agility. This cosmic alignment encourages you to explore the depths of your psyche, communicate with clarity and depth, and adapt to changing circumstances with ease. It's a time to embrace intellectual challenges, express your thoughts with honesty and authenticity, and embrace the transformative power of knowledge and understanding.

1 Thursday

With the Sun in Libra transiting your sixth house, your focus is on work, health, and daily routines. This period encourages you to establish balanced and harmonious habits that promote your well-being and productivity. You may feel more inclined to organize your workspace and prioritize tasks that enhance your professional life. Use this time to review and improve your health routines, ensuring that they support your overall vitality.

2 Friday

As Mercury forms a square with Pluto at 4:42 PM, there may be intense or transformative communications, power struggles, or a desire to uncover hidden truths. This aspect can bring about deep insights, but it's essential to approach conversations with honesty, integrity, and a willingness to listen. Avoid manipulation, control tactics, or obsessive thinking, and instead, focus on finding constructive solutions and fostering authentic connections.

3 Saturday

At 6:38 AM, Mars opposes Pluto, creating a powerful and potentially intense dynamic in the cosmic energies. This aspect can bring confrontations, power struggles, and challenges related to control and authority. It's essential to navigate this energy with caution, avoiding impulsive actions or manipulative behaviors. Use this time to confront underlying tensions, transform destructive patterns, and assert your boundaries with integrity and empathy.

4 Sunday

Overall, today's astrological influences encourage a balance between responsibility and self-expression. Embrace the lessons of the Sun-Saturn opposition by staying committed to your goals and duties while also allowing the Leo Moon to inspire confidence, creativity, and a joyful approach to life. Find ways to express yourself authentically, overcome challenges with determination, and celebrate your achievements along the way.

5 Monday

Many changes in your life help you improve your bottom line. It offers new possibilities and generates a great deal of forwarding momentum in your life. You shift away from outworn areas and discover the hidden blessings in learning and advancing your talents. Being proactive draws dividends as you climb the ladder to a new level of success in your working life. As you zoom toward new possibilities, you open a prosperous path ahead.

6 Tuesday

As the Moon enters Virgo, embrace a practical and organized approach to your daily life. Focus on tasks that require attention to detail, efficiency, and systematic planning. Use the Virgo Moon's energy to improve your routines, declutter your environment, and prioritize self-care practices that contribute to your well-being. Pay attention to your physical health, dietary habits, and overall lifestyle choices during this time.

7 Wednesday

Enjoy the dynamic and electric energy of the Mars sextile Uranus aspect as a catalyst for personal and collective growth. Trust in your instincts, be open to new experiences, and harness the power of innovation and creativity to propel you forward on your path. Use this cosmic alignment to break through limitations, embrace spontaneity, and ignite your inner fire for exciting new beginnings. Stay adaptable, remain open-minded, and be ready to seize opportunities.

8 Thursday

The Sun in Libra in the sixth house enhances your ability to manage your daily responsibilities with a sense of balance and fairness. You're likely to be more attentive to your health and work routines, making it an excellent time to implement positive changes. This influence can bring about a period of personal growth as you focus on creating a balanced and healthy lifestyle. By staying proactive in your daily tasks, you can make a more productive and fulfilling life.

9 Friday

The Moon's ingress into Libra at 4:10 AM marks a shift towards harmony, balance, and a focus on relationships and partnerships. Libra, represented by the scales, seeks equilibrium and fairness in all interactions, making this lunar transit an ideal time for fostering diplomacy, cooperation, and mutual understanding. This period encourages you to find common ground, promote harmony, and prioritize healthy connections with those around you.

10 Saturday

Venus forms a square aspect with Mars, creating a dynamic tension between love, desire, and assertiveness. This aspect may bring challenges in relationships, conflicts between needs and wants, or a heightened sense of passion and intensity. It's crucial to find a balance between expressing your desires and respecting the boundaries and needs of others. Use this energy to navigate relationship dynamics with honesty, assertiveness, and a willingness to find compromise.

11 Sunday

Under the influence of the Scorpio Moon, you may feel a strong pull towards uncovering hidden truths and exploring your innermost desires. This lunar ingress invites you to embrace vulnerability, confront deep-seated emotions, and embark on a journey of self-discovery. Use this time to connect with your inner strength and embrace the process of transformation. Allow yourself to release any emotional baggage that no longer serves you, making space for new beginnings.

12 Monday

The cosmic tides are turning in your favor, urging you to take a closer look at your financial health and make strategic decisions for long-term stability. It is a perfect time to revisit your budget, explore new investment opportunities, or seek advice from financial experts. With the universe supporting your monetary endeavors, you can build a solid foundation that promises security and prosperity. Trust the cosmic energy to guide you toward financial wisdom and abundance.

13 Tuesday

Under the influence of the Sagittarius Moon, you may feel a strong desire to break free from limitations and seek out new adventures. This lunar ingress invites you to embrace spontaneity, take calculated risks, and follow your passions with enthusiasm. Use this time to expand your horizons, step outside of your comfort zone, and pursue activities that ignite your sense of adventure, reminding yourself that life is full of surprises and possibilities.

14 Wednesday

Mercury in Scorpio in the seventh house sharpens your ability to negotiate and collaborate effectively with partners. You may feel more driven to achieve relationship goals through focused and well-thought-out efforts. Embrace this opportunity to transform your partnership dynamics, creating connections that are both profound and resilient. Your probing approach will help resolve underlying issues, making your relationships more authentic and fulfilling.

15 Thursday

Under the influence of the Sun-Jupiter sextile, you may feel a sense of confidence, optimism, and a desire to broaden your horizons. This celestial alignment encourages you to seize opportunities, take calculated risks, and pursue your goals with enthusiasm and determination. Use this time to expand your knowledge, explore new possibilities, and embrace a positive mindset that empowers you to manifest your dreams.

16 Friday

Under the influence of the Mars-Saturn trine, you may feel a strong sense of purpose, focus, and motivation to achieve your ambitions. This celestial alignment encourages you to work diligently, follow through with commitments, and utilize your energy and resources wisely. Use this time to establish solid routines, set realistic goals, and make steady progress toward your aspirations, leveraging your determination and persistence for meaningful outcomes.

17 Saturday

With Mars in Leo transiting your fourth house, your approach to home and family matters becomes more passionate and protective. This period encourages you to create a warm and dynamic domestic environment through bold and creative actions. You may find yourself more willing to invest in home improvements and family activities that bring joy and pride. It is a time to channel your energy into building a loving and vibrant household.

18 Sunday

The combination of the First Quarter Moon and the Moon's ingress into Aquarius encourages you to take proactive steps toward your goals while also fostering a sense of community and cooperation. Trust in your abilities, stay open to new perspectives and leverage the supportive energies to make progress both personally and collectively, knowing that your contributions have the potential to create positive change and inspire others to do the same.

19 Monday

The universe is opening doors for profound self-discovery and personal transformation. It is an influential period for introspection, where you can delve deep into your beliefs, values, and desires. Embrace this journey with an open heart and mind, and you will uncover new facets of yourself that lead to greater fulfillment and purpose. The celestial energies are aligning to support your growth, helping you emerge stronger and wiser.

20 Tuesday

When Venus forms a square with Pluto at 2:57 AM, intense emotions and power struggles may arise in relationships and matters of love and finances. This aspect can bring about deep transformations and challenges related to trust, control, and hidden desires. It's essential to navigate this energy with awareness and sensitivity, avoiding power struggles and manipulation and instead focusing on mutual understanding and growth.

21 Wednesday

The Sun's sextile with the South Node at 6:34 AM invites reflection on past experiences, lessons learned, and karmic patterns that may need addressing. This aspect encourages you to integrate wisdom from the past while also embracing new opportunities for growth and transformation. Embrace this opportunity to release outdated patterns and habits that no longer serve your growth, making room for new and positive experiences.

22 Thursday

Celestial influences highlight the importance of holistic health and wellness. Now is the time to focus on your physical, mental, and emotional well-being. Incorporate regular exercise, balanced nutrition, and mindfulness practices into your routine to enhance your overall health. The stars are supporting your efforts to achieve a harmonious balance in your life, promoting vitality, energy, and inner peace.

23 Friday

The combination of the Sun's ingress into Scorpio, the Moon's ingress into Aries, and the Sun's conjunction with Venus creates a dynamic and transformative energy that encourages personal growth, assertiveness, and meaningful connections. Embrace the depth of your emotions, take bold action toward your desires, and nurture loving relationships as you navigate this cosmic dance of intensity and harmony. Trust in your wisdom and follow your heart's desires.

24 Saturday

Mercury retrograde periods are known for potential challenges in communication, technology, and travel, so it's essential to exercise caution, double-check details, and be patient with delays or misunderstandings that may arise. Take this time to dive deep into your inner dialogue, explore new perspectives, and communicate with clarity and compassion. Embrace the retrograde energy as a chance to fine-tune your communication style and strengthen your connections with others.

25 Sunday

With Venus in Libra and the Moon in Taurus, there's a harmonious blend of beauty, comfort, and emotional stability. This alignment encourages you to appreciate the finer things in life, surround yourself with beauty and comfort, and cultivate a sense of inner peace and contentment. Take this opportunity to deepen your connections with loved ones, express your affection and appreciation, and create a nurturing environment that supports your well-being and happiness.

26 Monday

Following the Full Moon, the Sun engages in a dynamic square with Pluto, sparking intense energies related to power dynamics, transformation, and deep introspection. This aspect brings forth themes of personal empowerment, confronting inner shadows, and catalyzing change in areas of your life that may be stagnant or in need of transformation. The potent energies of this square can act as catalysts for growth, resilience, and a deeper understanding of your strength.

27 Tuesday

The Gemini Moon's influence encourages you to stay open-minded, explore different viewpoints, and seek mental stimulation through various activities. Use this time to engage in stimulating conversations, delve into topics that pique your interest, and sharpen your communication skills. Enjoy the versatility of Gemini energy as you navigate dynamic social interactions and engage in activities that challenge and inspire your intellect.

28 Wednesday

Celestial influences are prompting you to embrace the power of self-love and self-care, encouraging you to prioritize your well-being and nurture yourself on all levels – body, mind, and spirit. It is a time for practicing self-care rituals, setting healthy boundaries, and honoring your needs and desires. The universe supports your journey of self-love, guiding you toward opportunities for healing and personal growth.

29 Thursday

The Moon transitions into Cancer, infusing the atmosphere with nurturing, emotional sensitivity, and a solid connection for home and family. This lunar ingress invites you to prioritize your emotional well-being, seek comfort and security, and nurture your relationships with care and compassion. Embrace the soothing and protective energy of Cancer, allowing it to envelop you in a sense of emotional security and provide a nurturing foundation for your endeavors.

NOVEMBER

Mon	Tue	Wed	Thu	Fri	Sat	Sun
						1
2	3	4	5	6	7	8
9	10	11	12	13	14	15
16	17	18	19	20	21	22
23	24	25	26	27	28	29
30						

NEW MOON

_____

_____

_____

_____

_____

_____

_____

_____

_____

_____

_____

_____

_____

_____

_____

_____

_____

_____

_____

_____

_____

BEAVER MOON

30 Friday

Later in the day, at 6:13 PM, Venus forms a harmonious trine with the North Node and a supportive sextile with the South Node simultaneously, highlighting themes of destiny, growth, and karmic connections in relationships. This celestial dance encourages you to embrace positive developments in your love life, creative pursuits, and social interactions, fostering harmony and mutual understanding. Simultaneously, it releases old patterns and beliefs that no longer align.

31 Saturday

Saturn in Aries in the twelfth house challenges you to confront your deepest fears and limitations and to take responsibility for your spiritual growth and emotional well-being. You may feel a sense of heaviness or restriction as you encounter the darker aspects of your psyche, but these challenges are ultimately opportunities for healing and transformation. By embracing the process of inner work with discipline and determination, you can release old patterns and emerge stronger.

1 Sunday

At 12:18 AM, the Moon gracefully enters Leo, infusing the atmosphere with creativity, confidence, and a vibrant energy that encourages self-expression and boldness. This lunar ingress invites you to embrace your unique talents, tap into your creative potential, and share your passions with enthusiasm and authenticity, inspiring those around you with your radiant presence and igniting a sense of joy and love in your endeavors.

2 Monday

With the Sun in Scorpio transiting your seventh house, your focus is on relationships, partnerships, and one-on-one interactions. This period encourages you to dive deeply into your connections, seeking to understand the underlying dynamics and foster more profound bonds. You may feel more inclined to address issues in your relationships with honesty and intensity. Use this time to transform your partnerships by embracing vulnerability and authenticity.

3 Tuesday

With the Moon in Virgo, you may feel a heightened sense of diligence and a desire to analyze and improve various aspects of your life. It's a reasonable time for setting clear goals, mapping out strategies, and implementing practical solutions that enhance your well-being and effectiveness in achieving your objectives. Take advantage of this analytical energy to assess your routines, make necessary adjustments, and focus on tasks that contribute to your long-term goals.

4 Wednesday

At 9:24 AM, the Sun aligns with Mercury in conjunction, amplifying mental clarity, communication skills, and the ability to express yourself with confidence and precision. This celestial alignment enhances your intellect, supports transparent decision-making processes, and facilitates productive exchanges of ideas and information, allowing for meaningful insights and effective problem-solving. Utilize this alignment to engage in fruitful discussions.

5 Thursday

Under the influence of the Libra Moon, you may feel more inclined to prioritize harmony, seek compromises, and strive for consensus in your interactions. This lunar ingress invites you to approach conflicts with grace, practice active listening, and find common ground that honors the needs and perspectives of all parties involved. Embrace this time as an opportunity to cultivate healthy communication, empathy, and a sense of unity in your relationships.

6 Friday

With Jupiter in Leo transiting your fourth house, your focus is on home, family, and emotional foundations. This period encourages you to create a warm and supportive home environment that fosters growth and happiness. You may feel more inclined to invest in your living space and strengthen family bonds. Use this time to enhance your domestic life and nurture your well-being. A generous approach to home and family helps you create a harmonious environment.

7 Saturday

When the Moon transitions into Scorpio at 5:40 PM, an intense energy permeates the atmosphere, encouraging introspection, emotional depth, and transformation. The Scorpio Moon invites you to explore the hidden realms of your psyche, confront deep-seated emotions, and embrace authenticity in your interactions and experiences. This lunar ingress heralds a period of deep introspection and emotional exploration, urging you to delve beneath the surface.

8 Sunday

The Sun in Scorpio in the seventh house enhances your ability to engage with others in a deep and meaningful way. You're likely to be more focused on understanding your partners and working through any challenges together. This influence can bring about a period of relational growth as you navigate the complexities of your interactions. By committing to open communication, you can achieve greater harmony and intimacy in your relationships.

9 Monday

the New Moon encourages you to embrace a sense of optimism, courage, and willingness to take inspired action. Step out of your comfort zone, embrace new opportunities, and believe in your ability to create positive change. Use this time to cultivate a mindset of abundance, possibility, and empowerment, knowing that you have the power to shape reality and grow your dreams. Trust in the universe's support and take intentional steps towards manifesting your heart's desires.

10 Tuesday

Today's astrological influences of Venus, sextile Mars, and the Moon in Sagittarius create an atmosphere ripe for passion, creativity, and adventurous exploration. Embrace the harmonious energy between Venus and Mars to nurture relationships and express your desires with confidence. Allow the Sagittarius Moon's influence to ignite adventure, curiosity, and optimism, leading you toward new experiences and opportunities for personal and spiritual growth.

11 Wednesday

In the heart of social gatherings, where the air is alive with the buzz of conversation and the energy of shared experiences, there's a sense of kinship that binds you together with kindred spirits. It's a time when your heart swells with the joy of connection, when every smile is a beacon of warmth and acceptance, and when the bonds of friendship deepen with every shared moment. So, let yourself revel in the magic of social interactions.

12 Thursday

Under the influence of Jupiter's aspects on the lunar nodes, you may experience a push-pull effect between embracing new opportunities for growth and addressing unresolved issues from the past. It's essential to find a balance between expansion and consolidation, integrating past experiences while also moving forward with optimism and purpose. Use this astrological influence as an opportunity to reflect on your path and release outdated beliefs or habits.

13 Friday

The direct motion of Mercury and Venus encourages you to embrace clarity, open communication, and harmony in your interactions and relationships. It's a favorable time for initiating essential conversations, making romantic gestures, and expressing your appreciation for loved ones. Use this cosmic energy to strengthen connections, resolve misunderstandings, and cultivate loving and harmonious dynamics in your personal and professional life.

14 Saturday

Today's astrological influences of Mars opposing the North Node and conjuncting the South Node invite you to embrace conscious action, self-awareness, and alignment with your soul's path. Use this time to confront old patterns, assert yourself in a balanced and purposeful manner, and take steps toward fulfilling your destiny with courage, integrity, and determination. Trust in the process of growth and transformation, and embrace the opportunities for empowerment.

15 Sunday

As the Moon ingresses into Aquarius at 4:24 AM, it heralds a shift towards a more detached and intellectual approach to emotions. You may find yourself drawn to unconventional perspectives, humanitarian causes, or innovative ideas during this transit. The influence of Aquarius encourages you to step back emotionally and view situations from a broader, more objective viewpoint. It's a favorable time for group activities and socializing with like-minded individuals.

16 Monday

The Mars-Jupiter conjunction inspires you to pursue your ambitions with vigor. It boosts your courage, initiative, and willingness to take risks in order to reach new heights of success. This alignment favors endeavors that require courage, leadership, and a pioneering spirit. It's a time to embrace challenges, think big, and strive for excellence in all your endeavors. Remember to channel this energy into projects that align with your long-term vision and values.

17 Tuesday

At 8:13 AM, the Sun squares both the North Node and the South Node, creating a tense aspect that emphasizes karmic lessons and life path adjustments. The Sun square North Node challenges you to step out of your comfort zone and align with your soul's purpose, while the Sun square South Node urges you to release old patterns and beliefs that no longer serve your growth. This cosmic alignment may bring significant insights into your past and present.

18 Wednesday

When the Sun squares Jupiter at 4:38 AM, it signals a clash between expansive energy and the need for moderation. This aspect can bring a sense of overconfidence or exaggeration, prompting caution in decision-making and planning. It's essential to balance optimism with realism and avoid overextending yourself or taking on too much at once, as this alignment may highlight areas where a more measured approach is necessary.

19 Thursday

The square between the Sun and Mars challenges you to find a balance between assertiveness and diplomacy, encouraging you to assert your boundaries assertively while also being mindful of others' perspectives. While Mars fuels your drive, ambition, and determination, the square from the Sun may highlight areas where you need to temper aggression or impulsiveness, reminding you to approach conflicts with a level-headed attitude and open communication.

20 Friday

The Moon's ingress into Aries can inspire a surge of energy and motivation, making it an excellent time to initiate new projects, start afresh, and tackle obstacles with a proactive mindset, fueling your drive to overcome the barriers and make progress. However, it's important to temper this newfound assertiveness with patience and consideration for others, recognizing that diplomacy and collaboration can also lead to successful outcomes.

21 Saturday

Celestial influences stir a sense of adventure within your soul, urging you to explore new horizons and embrace the unknown with courage and curiosity. This cosmic stirring is a time for stepping out of your comfort zone, taking risks, and embarking on exciting new adventures. The universe supports your journey of exploration, guiding you toward experiences that expand your consciousness and elevate your spirit.

22 Sunday

The Moon ingresses into your sign, shifting the emotional focus towards stability, comfort, and sensuality. Taurus, ruled by Venus, emphasizes pleasure, security, and the enjoyment of life's simple pleasures. This lunar transit encourages you to connect with your senses, indulge in self-care, and create a harmonious environment that nurtures your well-being. It's a joyful time for enjoying physical comforts, savoring delicious meals, and surrounding yourself with tranquility.

23 Monday

The Sun forms a trine aspect with Neptune, infusing your day with creativity, inspiration, and spiritual insights. This aspect enhances your intuition, imagination, and empathy, making it a favorable time for artistic endeavors, spiritual practices, and connecting with your higher self. It's a period for tapping into your inner wisdom and aligning with your dreams and ideals, allowing you to express yourself authentically and manifest your visions with clarity and grace.

24 Tuesday

The combination of the Moon's ingress into Gemini and the Full Moon creates a dynamic and expressive energy. It's a time for communication, sharing ideas, and connecting with others on a mental level. Embrace opportunities for learning, networking, and creative expression while also honoring your emotional insights and inner wisdom during this significant lunar event. Allow the synergy of Gemini's curiosity and the Full Moon's illumination to inspire new horizons.

25 Wednesday

At 5:41 PM, the Sun opposes Uranus, creating a dynamic and potentially disruptive energy. This aspect can bring unexpected events, sudden changes, and a desire for freedom and independence. It's a time to expect the unexpected, adapt to new situations, and remain flexible in your approach to challenges. Embrace the opportunity for innovation and breakthroughs, but stay mindful of impulsivity and the need for balance amidst change.

26 Thursday

When the Moon ingresses into Cancer at 5:51 AM, it brings a shift in emotional focus towards nurturing, sensitivity, and home life. Cancer, ruled by the Moon itself, emphasizes emotions, intuition, and a need for security and comfort. This lunar transit encourages you to prioritize your emotional well-being, connect with loved ones, and create a supportive and cozy environment. Take this opportunity to nurture yourself and those around you, finding solace in familiar surroundings.

27 Friday

Jupiter in Leo in the fourth house enhances your ability to create a loving and joyful home atmosphere, making it a sanctuary for yourself and your loved ones. You are likely to be more focused on building strong family connections and creating a stable and nurturing foundation. This influence can bring about a period of emotional growth and domestic happiness as you invest in your home and relationships.

28 Saturday

When the Moon ingresses into Leo at 6:20 AM, it ushers in a period of heightened passion, creativity, and self-expression. Leo, ruled by the Sun, encourages confidence, playfulness, and a desire to shine. This lunar transit invites you to embrace your unique talents, showcase your personality, and engage in activities that bring joy and excitement. It's a time to step into the spotlight, express yourself boldly, and share your creative gifts with the world.

29 Sunday

The Uranus trine Pluto aspect encourages you to embrace your authentic self, break free from limitations, and pursue your goals with confidence and determination. It supports unconventional approaches, creative solutions, and a willingness to explore new territories. Use this transformative energy to make positive changes, align with your true purpose, and manifest your vision. Embrace your unique talents, and trust in your ability to navigate change with courage.

DECEMBER

Mon	Tue	Wed	Thu	Fri	Sat	Sun
	1	2	3	4	5	6
7	8	9	10	11	12	13
14	15	16	17	18	19	20
21	22	23	24	25	26	27
28	29	30	31			

NEW MOON

_____

_____

_____

_____

_____

_____

_____

_____

_____

_____

_____

_____

_____

_____

_____

_____

_____

_____

_____

_____

COLD MOON

30 Monday

When the Sun forms a trine aspect with Saturn at 1:05 AM, it brings a harmonious alignment between discipline, structure, and personal growth. This aspect encourages a sense of stability, responsibility, and long-term planning. It's a favorable time for making practical decisions, setting achievable goals, and laying solid foundations for future success. Use this supportive energy to create a roadmap for your ambitions and commit to the steps needed to achieve them.

1 Tuesday

Mercury's square to your North Node brings a dynamic tension between communication, intellect, and your karmic path. The North Node represents the direction of growth and evolution in your life, while Mercury governs your thoughts and how you express them. This aspect challenges you to confront any discrepancies between your communication style and your higher purpose, urging you to communicate with clarity and integrity as you navigate your destined path.

2 Wednesday

The Moon gracefully transitions into Libra, marking a shift in emotional focus towards harmony, balance, and diplomacy. Libra, ruled by Venus, invites you to seek beauty and harmony in your surroundings, fostering a desire for fairness and cooperation in your interactions. Under this lunar influence, relationships take center stage as you strive to promote mutual understanding. This ingress encourages you to approach challenges with a diplomatic mindset.

3 Thursday

With the Sun in Sagittarius shining its light on your eighth house, your focus turns to transformation, intimacy, and shared resources. This period encourages you to embrace change with optimism and openness, trusting in the process of growth and evolution. You may feel a strong desire to delve deep into your psyche, confront your fears, and release any emotional baggage that is holding you back. Use this time to explore new avenues for personal growth.

4 Friday

You may feel the tension as Mercury squares Jupiter, challenging your thoughts and communication. This aspect can lead to exaggerated ideas or promises, so it's crucial to maintain a balanced perspective and avoid overcommitting or taking on too much. Be mindful of potential misunderstandings or conflicts arising from differences in opinions or beliefs, and strive to communicate with clarity and honesty to navigate this aspect effectively while staying grounded in reality.

5 Saturday

With Mars in Virgo transiting your fifth house, your approach to creativity, romance, and recreation becomes more practical and detail-oriented. This period encourages you to pursue your passions and desires with precision and a systematic approach, focusing on activities that require careful planning and execution. You may find yourself more willing to take on creative projects that benefit from meticulous attention to detail.

6 Sunday

As Mercury journeys through Sagittarius, you are encouraged to embrace a spirit of intellectual curiosity and open-mindedness. It is a time for exploration, expansion, and growth, both intellectually and spiritually. You may find yourself drawn to opportunities for learning and discovery as you seek out new experiences and expand your horizons. This transit encourages you to embrace the unknown with enthusiasm and optimism, trusting in the journey.

7 Monday

At 3:35 AM, the Moon gracefully enters Sagittarius, ushering in a shift towards expansive thinking, exploration, and philosophical inquiry. In Sagittarius, Mercury encourages you to broaden your horizons, embrace new perspectives, and embark on a quest for knowledge and understanding. This transit ignites a spirit of curiosity and adventure, inspiring you to explore diverse ideas, cultures, and belief systems with enthusiasm and optimism.

8 Tuesday

At 2:31 PM, Mercury forms a harmonious sextile with Pluto, deepening your understanding and insight into complex matters. This aspect enhances your powers of perception and intuition, allowing you to penetrate beneath the surface and uncover hidden truths. It's a favorable time for research, investigation, or delving into psychological or metaphysical subjects. Your words carry a profound impact now, enabling you to communicate with depth and conviction.

9 Wednesday

Venus squares Pluto, intensifying emotions and relationships. This aspect may bring power struggles, jealousy, or control issues to the surface in your romantic or financial dealings. Be mindful of hidden agendas, and strive for honesty and transparency in your interactions. It's essential to address any underlying issues or insecurities with compassion and empathy, as this transit offers an opportunity for profound transformation and healing in your relationships.

10 Thursday

At 7 PM, a significant celestial event unfolds as Saturn, the cosmic taskmaster and planet of discipline and structure, resumes its forward motion after a period of retrograde. Saturn's direct movement carries profound implications, marking a pivotal moment of clarity and progress in your collective journey. This shift signals a time when the lessons and challenges presented during Saturn's retrograde phase begin to crystallize into tangible outcomes and forward momentum.

11 Friday

The rare celestial dance between Mercury and Saturn creates a conducive environment for practical endeavors and strategic planning. It's as if the universe has granted you access to a wellspring of wisdom and foresight, enabling you to approach tasks with a methodical mindset and a keen eye for detail. Whether you're organizing your schedule, solving intricate problems, or engaging in meaningful discussions, you'll find that your decision-making is sound.

12 Saturday

At 6:11 PM, Neptune, the planet of dreams and illusions, stations directly, signaling a time of increased clarity and spiritual insight. After several months of retrograde motion, Neptune's direct movement encourages you to trust your intuition and tap into your innate wisdom. This cosmic shift invites you to embrace your imagination and creativity as you navigate the realm of dreams and subconscious desires with newfound clarity and purpose.

13 Sunday

Mercury in Sagittarius in the eighth house enhances your ability to handle complex issues related to shared resources and intimacy with optimism and insight. You may feel more driven to achieve transformation and growth through focused and well-thought-out efforts. Embrace this opportunity to refine your approach to shared responsibilities, creating a balanced and equitable environment. Your problem-solving skills can lead to increased trust.

14 Monday

By 11:35 PM, the Moon gracefully transitions into Pisces, infusing the atmosphere with dreamy, imaginative energy. Pisces, ruled by Neptune, encourages introspection, empathy, and connection to the mystical realms. Under this lunar influence, you may find yourself more attuned to your emotions, intuition, and spiritual insights. It is a favorable time for creative expression, meditation, and exploring the depths of your subconscious mind.

15 Tuesday

In the eighth house, the Sun in Sagittarius inspires you to embrace the transformative power of change with optimism and enthusiasm. You may feel a sense of adventure and curiosity as you explore the hidden aspects of your psyche and confront your deepest fears and desires. This influence encourages you to trust in the process of regeneration and to embrace the opportunities for growth that arise from letting go of old patterns and beliefs.

16 Wednesday

The universe weaves a tapestry of abundance, showering you with blessings and opportunities to thrive. It is a time for embracing the prosperity that surrounds you, opening your heart to abundance, and welcoming wealth into your life with gratitude and joy. The celestial energies support your journey toward financial and material prosperity, guiding you toward opportunities that align with your highest good.

17 Thursday

The lunar phase transitions to the First Quarter, marking a pivotal moment in the lunar cycle. This phase invites you to overcome any challenges or obstacles that have arisen since the New Moon. The First Quarter Moon encourages you to assert yourself and move forward with confidence as you work towards manifesting your intentions and goals for the month ahead. It's a time for decision-making, initiative, and taking the necessary steps to turn your dreams into reality.

18 Friday

The Sun-Jupiter trine invites you to dream big and set your sights on ambitious goals, knowing that the universe supports your endeavors. It is a time for taking calculated risks, exploring new horizons, and embracing opportunities for growth and expansion. Trust in your ability to manifest your dreams and cultivate abundance in all areas of your life. This alignment empowers you to step into your power and create a brighter future.

19 Saturday

Embrace the grounded and earthy energy of Taurus as you navigate the day, knowing that you are supported in creating a sense of stability and security in your life. Trust in the wisdom of your body and intuition to guide you towards greater peace and fulfillment, and allow yourself to revel in the abundance and beauty that surrounds you. With the Moon in Taurus, you're reminded to appreciate the simple joys of life and to find comfort and solace in the present moment.

20 Sunday

The Mercury-North Node sextile opens the doorway to new possibilities and potentials, inviting you to align your thoughts and communication with your highest path and purpose. This aspect facilitates clear and intuitive communication, making it an excellent time for sharing ideas, making plans, or engaging in meaningful conversations that support your growth and evolution. Pay attention to synchronicities that guide you toward opportunities.

21 Monday

The December Solstice marks a significant astronomical event, signaling the beginning of winter in the Northern Hemisphere and summer in the Southern Hemisphere. This celestial phenomenon heralds the shortest day and longest night of the year, inviting you to turn inward and embrace the reflective energy of the season. It's a time for reflection, renewal, and setting intentions for the cycle ahead as you honor the rhythm of nature and the changing of the seasons.

22 Tuesday

The cosmos aligns to create a sense of togetherness and unity among loved ones during this Christmas week, fostering deep connections and heartfelt bonds. It is a time for gathering with family and friends, sharing stories and laughter, and creating cherished memories that will last a lifetime. The universe supports your sense of belonging, guiding you toward opportunities for connection, camaraderie, and mutual support.

23 Wednesday

Midday arrives with a harmonious alignment between the messenger planet Mercury and the expansive Jupiter, bestowing upon you a gift of clarity, optimism, and boundless potential. Your thoughts may soar to new heights as you tap into the wellspring of knowledge and wisdom within. It is a time for intellectual growth, open-mindedness, and expansive thinking. Seize the opportunity to broaden your horizons and communicate with confidence.

24 Thursday

As the clock strikes midnight and Christmas Day dawns, you know that this moment – this magical, enchanting moment – is one that you will always carry with you. For on this night, in this moment, you are reminded of the true meaning of Christmas – the gift of love, the joy of togetherness, and the promise of hope for the future. And as you bask in the warmth of this beautiful holiday, you know that you are truly blessed.

25 Friday

Later in the afternoon, the moon ingresses into Leo at 4:12 PM, infusing your emotions with a fiery and expressive energy. You may feel a heightened sense of passion, creativity, and self-confidence during this time. Embrace your inner lion or lioness and allow yourself to shine brightly in the spotlight. This transit encourages you to express yourself authentically, follow your heart's desires, and seek out opportunities for joy and self-expression.

26 Saturday

In the dance between the planet of intellect and the nebulous depths of Neptune, it becomes crucial to anchor yourself in discernment and clarity. Trust in your inner wisdom to navigate through any murky waters that may arise, allowing intuition to serve as your guiding light amidst the shadows. Embrace the opportunity to cultivate a deeper understanding of truth amidst the veils of illusion that Neptune may cast, recognizing the power of perception in shaping reality.

27 Sunday

Amidst the precision of Virgo's domain, there lies an opportunity for healing and self-care. Take this time to nurture your body, mind, and spirit, attending to your physical, emotional, and spiritual needs with loving attention. Engage in practices that promote health and well-being, such as mindfulness meditation, gentle exercise, and nourishing meals. Honor the interconnectedness of all aspects of your being and seek to cultivate wholeness and alignment within yourself.

28 Monday

With Saturn in Aries transiting your twelfth house, your focus is on spiritual growth, introspection, and subconscious patterns. This period encourages you to approach your inner world with discipline, patience, and a willingness to confront your deepest fears and limitations. You may encounter challenges or obstacles in your spiritual practice or inner journey, but these challenges are opportunities for growth and self-discovery.

29 Tuesday

As Venus forms challenging squares with both the North Node and the South Node at 4:42 PM, you may feel a tug-of-war between the past and the future in matters of love, relationships, and values. These aspects urge you to confront any lingering karmic patterns or unresolved issues from the past that may be hindering your growth. Embrace this opportunity to release old attachments and step into alignment with your soul's evolutionary path.

30 Wednesday

At 6:54 PM, Mercury squares Saturn, casting a serious tone over communication and mental processes. You may encounter challenges in expressing yourself effectively or experiencing delays in matters of logistics or decision-making. Approach tasks with patience and diligence, trusting that obstacles are opportunities for growth. Use this aspect as a catalyst for disciplined focus and structured thinking, knowing that perseverance will lead to eventual success.

31 Thursday

In the radiance of today's cosmic alignments, embrace the fiery spirit of Mars as it ignites your soul with courage and determination. Allow the illuminating influence of the Sun and the sharp intellect of Mercury to guide your actions and communications with purpose and clarity. With passion as your fuel and clarity as your compass, you are poised to conquer any obstacles and achieve your aspirations with grace and resilience.

2026 List of Astrological Events

The time zone is America Eastern Time, EST. The GMT offset is -5:00.

January

Thursday 1st
Sun sextile North Node 5:22 AM
Sun trine South Node at 5:22 AM
Mercury Square Neptune 8:33 AM
Mercury ingress Capricorn 4:12 PM
Friday 2nd
Venus sextile North Node 2:27 AM
Venus trine South Node 2:27 AM
Moon ingress Cancer 8:09 AM
Saturday 3rd
Full Moon 5:04 AM
Sunday 4th
Moon ingress Leo 8:43 AM
Tuesday 6th
Moon ingress Virgo 11:56 AM
Thursday 8th
Mercury sextile North Node 7:07 AM
Mercury trine South Node 7:07 AM
Moon ingress Libra 7:06 PM
Friday 9th
Venus opposed Jupiter 12:34 PM
Saturday 10th
Sun opposed Jupiter 3:42 AM
Mars opposed Jupiter at 9:25 AM
Moon last Quarter at 10:49 AM
Sunday 11th
Moon ingress Scorpio 5:55 AM
Tuesday 13th
Moon ingress Sagittarius 6:34 PM
Wednesday 14th
Mercury opposed Jupiter at 3:17 AM
Thursday 15th
Venus sextile Saturn 1:18 AM
Venus trine Uranus 10:22 AM
Friday 16th

Moon ingress Capricorn 6:47 AM
Saturday 17th
Venus sextile Neptune 3:33 AM
Sun sextile Saturn 5:41 AM
Venus ingress Aquarius 7:45 AM
Sun trine Uranus 11:58 AM
Sunday 18th
New Moon 2:53 PM
Moon ingress Aquarius 5:18 PM
Mercury sextile Saturn 11:09 PM
Monday 19th
Mercury trine Uranus 12:37 AM
Sun sextile Neptune 4:54 PM
Sun ingress Aquarius 8:47 PM
Tuesday 20th
Saturn sextile Uranus 12:18 AM
Mars trine Uranus 12:56 AM
Mars sextile Saturn 1:01 AM
Mercury sextile Neptune 9:34 AM
Mercury ingress Aquarius 11:42 AM
Wednesday 21st
Moon ingress Pisces 1:49 AM
Friday 23rd
Mars sextile Neptune 1:39 AM
Mars ingress Aquarius 4:20 AM
Moon ingress Aries 8:25 AM
Sunday 25th
Moon ingress Taurus 1:05 PM
Moon first Quarter at 11:48 PM
Monday 26th
Neptune ingress Aries 2:16 PM
Tuesday 27th
Moon ingress Gemini 3:55 PM
Thursday 29th
Moon ingress Cancer 5:31 PM
Saturday 31st
Moon ingress Leo 7:09 PM

February

Sunday 1st
Full Moon 5:10 PM
Monday 2nd
Moon ingress Virgo 10:21 PM
Tuesday 3rd
Uranus turns direct at 8:53 PM
Thursday 5th
Moon ingress Libra 4:32 AM
Mercury square Uranus 7:13 AM
Friday 6th
Mercury ingress Pisces 5:49 PM
Saturday 7th
Moon ingress Scorpio 2:13 PM
Sunday 8th
Venus Square Uranus 4:48 AM
Monday 9th
Moon last Quarter 7:44 AM
Tuesday 10th
Moon ingress Sagittarius 2:22 AM
Venus ingress Pisces 5:20 AM
Thursday 12th
Mercury opposed South Node 1:17 AM
Moon ingress Capricorn 2:44 PM
Friday 13th
Saturn ingress Aries 7:37 PM
Sunday 15th
Moon ingress Aquarius 1:16 AM

Monday 16th
Sun square Uranus 12:01 AM
Mercury trine Jupiter 4:28 PM
Tuesday 17th
New Moon 7:02 AM
Venus opposed South node 7:45 AM
Moon ingress Pisces 9:09 AM
Wednesday 18th
Sun ingress Pisces 10:54 AM
Thursday 19th
Moon ingress Aries 2:39 PM
Saturday 21st
Moon ingress Taurus 6:31 PM
Sunday 22nd
Venus trine Jupiter 3:01 PM
Monday 23rd
Moon ingress Gemini 9:29 PM
Tuesday 24th
Moon First Quarter 7:28 AM
Thursday 26th
Moon ingress Cancer 12:11 AM
Mercury turns retrograde at 1:47 AM
Friday 27th
Sun opposed South Node 7:32 AM
Mars square Uranus 11:20 AM
Saturday 28th
Moon ingress Leo 3:17 AM

March

Monday 2nd
Moon ingress Virgo 7:34 AM
Mars ingress Pisces 9:19 AM
Tuesday 3rd
Full Moon 6:39 AM
Wednesday 4th
Venus sextile Uranus 11:40 AM
Moon ingress Libra 1:56 PM
Thursday 5th
Sun trine Jupiter 12:13 PM
Friday 6th
Venus ingress Aries 5:47 AM
Moon ingress Scorpio 11:01 PM
Monday 9th
Mercury trine Jupiter 1:22 AM
Moon ingress Sagittarius 11:36 AM
Tuesday 10th
Venus sextile Pluto 2:52 AM
Jupiter turns direct at 11:36 PM
Wednesday 11th
Moon last Quarter at 5:39 AM
Thursday 12th
Moon ingress Capricorn 12:07 AM
Friday 13th
Mars opposed South Node 4:52 PM
Saturday 14th
Moon ingress Aquarius 11:13 AM
Monday 16th
Moon ingress Pisces 7:15 PM
Tuesday 17th
Mercury opposed South Node 5 PM
Wednesday 18th

Venus square Jupiter 12:08 PM
Sun sextile Uranus 4:20 PM
New Moon 9:24 PM
Thursday 19th
Moon ingress Aries 12:03 AM
Friday 20th
Vernal March Equinox 10:47 AM
Sun ingress Aries 10:48 AM
Mercury turns direct at 3:32 PM
Saturday 21st
Moon ingress Taurus 2:35 AM
Mars trine Jupiter 8 PM
Sunday 22nd
Mercury opposed South Node 8:49 PM
Monday 23rd
Moon ingress Gemini 4:18 AM
Wednesday 25th
Moon ingress Cancer 6:33 AM
Sun sextile Pluto 2:16 PM
Moon first Quarter at 3:18 PM
Friday 27th
Moon ingress Leo 10:10 AM
Saturday 28th
Saturn sextile Pluto 6:10 PM
Sunday 29th
Moon ingress Virgo 3:33 PM
Monday 30th
Venus ingress Taurus 12:02 PM
Tuesday 31st
Moon ingress Libra 10:51 PM

April

Wednesday 1st
Full Moon 10:13 PM
Friday 3rd
Mercury trine Jupiter 7:30 AM
Moon ingress Scorpio 8:11 AM
Venus square Pluto 6:38 PM
Sunday 5th
Sun square Jupiter 6:22 PM
Moon ingress Sagittarius 7:31 PM
Monday 6th
Venus sextile North Node 5:47 AM
Venus trine South Node 5:47 AM
Wednesday 8th
Moon ingress Capricorn 8:04 AM
Mars sextile Uranus 12:11 PM
Thursday 9th
Mars ingress Aries 3:39 PM
Friday 10th
Moon last Quarter 12:52 AM
Moon ingress Aquarius 7:55 PM
Monday 13th
Venus sextile Jupiter 4:20 AM
Moon ingress Pisces 4:55 AM
Tuesday 14th
Mercury sextile Uranus 1:11 PM
Mercury ingress Aries 11:23 PM
Wednesday 15th
Moon ingress Aries 10:03 AM
Thursday 16th
Mars sextile Pluto 2:55 PM
Friday 17th
New Moon 7:52 AM

Moon ingress Taurus 11:57 AM
Saturday 18th
Mercury sextile Pluto 4:35 PM
Sunday 19th
Moon ingress Gemini 12:17 PM
Sun ingress Taurus 9:41 PM
Tuesday 21st
Moon ingress Cancer 1:00 PM
Thursday 23rd
Moon ingress Leo 3:41 PM
Moon First Quarter 10:32 PM
Friday 24th
Venus ingress Gemini 12:05 AM
Saturday 25th
Sun square Pluto 12:32 PM
Moon ingress Virgo 9:04 PM
Uranus ingress Gemini 9:35 PM
Sunday 26th
Venus sextile Neptune at 1:42 PM
Mercury Square Jupiter 2:33 PM
Monday 27th
Sun sextile North Node at 9:19 AM
Sun trine South Node at 9:19 AM
Tuesday 28th
Moon ingress Libra 5:03 AM
Venus trine Pluto 12:39 PM
Wednesday 29th
Venus Square North Node at 9:19 PM
Venus Square South Node at 9:19 PM
Thursday 30th
Moon ingress Scorpio 3:02 PM

May

Friday 1st
Full Moon 1:24 PM
Venus sextile Saturn 2:45 PM
Saturday 2nd
Mercury ingress Taurus 10:57 PM
Sunday 3rd
Moon ingress Sagittarius 2:33 AM
Monday 4th
Mars square Jupiter 10:08 PM
Tuesday 5th
Moon ingress Capricorn 3:06 PM
Mercury square Pluto 6:08 PM
Wednesday 6th
Mercury sextile North Node 2:06 AM
Mercury South Node 2:06 AM
Pluto turns retrograde at 10:14 AM
Friday 8th
Moon ingress Aquarius 3:27 AM
Saturday 9th
Moon Last Quarter 5:11 PM
Sunday 10th
Moon ingress Pisces 1:39 PM
Sun sextile Jupiter 10:13 PM
Tuesday 12th
Moon ingress Aries 8:03 PM
Wednesday 13th
Mercury sextile Jupiter 12:43 AM
Thursday 14th
Moon ingress Taurus 10:31 PM
Saturday 16th New Moon 4:02 PM
Moon ingress Gemini 10:23 PM
Sunday 17th
Mercury ingress Gemini 6:27 AM

Monday 18th
Mars ingress Taurus 6:28 PM
Venus ingress Cancer 9:07 PM
Moon ingress Cancer 9:46 PM
Tuesday 19th
Mercury sextile Neptune 12:04 AM
Venus sextile Mars 1:37 AM
Mercury Square North Node 12 PM
Mercury Square South Node 12 PM
Mercury trine Pluto 6:52 PM
Wednesday 20th
Sun ingress Gemini 8:39 PM
Moon ingress Leo 10:48 PM
Friday 22nd
Venus square Neptune 2:31 AM
Mercury sextile Saturn 2:02 PM
Venus trine North node 5:55 PM
Venus sextile South node 5:55 PM
Saturday 23rd
Moon ingress Virgo 2:57 AM
Moon First Quarter 7:12 AM
Sunday 24th
Mars sextile North Node 9:56 PM
Mars trine South Node 9:56 PM
Sun sextile Neptune 10:22 PM
Monday 25th
Moon ingress Libra 10:34 AM
Sun square North node 3:22 PM
Sun square South node 3:22 PM
Tuesday 26th
Mars square Pluto 12:01 AM
Sun trine Pluto 11:52 AM
Wednesday 27th
Moon ingress Scorpio 8:52 PM
Thursday 28th
Venus square Saturn at 11:02 PM

Saturday 30th
Moon ingress Sagittarius 8:45 AM

Sunday 31st
Full Moon 4:46 AM

June

Monday 1st
Mercury ingress Cancer 7:57 AM
Moon ingress Capricorn 9:19 PM
Tuesday 2nd
Sun sextile Saturn 6:48 PM
Wednesday 3rd
Mercury trine North Node 7:39 AM
Mercury sextile South Node 7:39 AM
Mercury Square Neptune 8:17 PM
Thursday 4th
Moon ingress Aquarius 9:45 AM
Saturday 6th
Moon ingress Pisces 8:42 PM
Monday 8th
Moon last Quarter 6:01 AM
Tuesday 9th
Moon ingress Aries 4:33 AM
Wednesday 10th
Mercury square Saturn 1:37 AM
Thursday 11th
Moon ingress Taurus 8:27 AM
Friday 12th
Uranus square North Node 2:43 PM
Uranus square South Node 2:43 PM
Saturday 13th
Venus ingress Leo 6:49 AM
Moon ingress Gemini 9:06 AM
Sunday 14th
New Moon 10:55 PM
Monday 15th
Moon ingress Cancer 8:14 AM
Venus sex tile Uranus 6:52 PM

Tuesday 16th
Venus trine Neptune at 11:40 PM
Wednesday 17th
Moon ingress Leo 8:05 AM
Venus opposed to Pluto 4:38 PM
Friday 19th
Moon ingress Virgo 10:37 AM
Sunday 21st
June Solstice 4:25 AM
Sun ingress Cancer 4:27 AM
Moon ingress Libra 4:55 PM
Moon first Quarter at 5:56 PM
Tuesday 23rd
Sun trine North node 2:09 AM
Sun sextile South node 2:09 AM
Wednesday 24th
Moon ingress Scorpio 2:43 AM
Thursday 25th
Venus trine Saturn 8:01 AM
Sun square Neptune 6:38 PM
Friday 26th
Moon ingress Sagittarius 2:41 PM
Sunday 28th
Mars sextile Jupiter 12:50 AM
Mars ingress Gemini 3:33 PM
Monday 29th
Moon ingress Capricorn 3:18 AM
Mercury turns retrograde at 1:35 PM
full Moon 7:57 PM
Tuesday 30th
Mars square North node 1:31 AM
Mars square South node 1:31 AM
Jupiter ingress Leo 2:07 AM

July

Wednesday 1st
Moon ingress Aquarius 3:33 PM
Saturday 4th
Moon ingress Pisces 2:30 AM
Mars sextile Neptune 8:44 PM
Sunday 5th
Mars trine Pluto 9:06 AM
Monday 6th
Sun square Saturn 6:47 AM
Moon ingress Aries 11:07 AM
Tuesday 7th
Neptune turns retro at 7:40 AM
Moon last Quarter 3:30 PM
Wednesday 8th
Moon ingress Taurus 4:30 PM
Thursday 9th
Venus ingress Virgo 1:25 PM
Friday 10th
Venus opposed North Node 4:20 AM
Moon ingress Gemini 6:41 PM
Sunday 12th
Moon ingress Cancer 6:46 PM
Monday 13th
Venus Square Uranus 10:26 AM
Tuesday 14th
New Moon 5:44 AM
Moon ingress Leo 6:35 PM
Wednesday 15th
Uranus sextile Neptune 4:35 PM
Thursday 16th
Moon ingress Virgo 8:07 PM
Saturday 18th
Uranus trine Pluto 12:43 AM

Sunday 19th
Moon ingress Libra 12:57 AM
Mars sextile Saturn 2:10 PM
Monday 20th
Jupiter trine Neptune 3:23 AM
Jupiter opposed Pluto at 10:44 AM
Tuesday 21st
Moon First Quarter 7:06 AM
Jupiter sextile Uranus 7:10 AM
Moon ingress Scorpio 9:35 AM
Wednesday 22nd
Sun ingress Leo 3:16 PM
Thursday 23rd
Mercury turns direct at 6:58 PM
Sagittarius 9:07 PM
Friday 24th
Mercury sextile Venus 12:08 PM
Saturday 25th
Neptune sextile Pluto 1:25 AM
Sunday 26th
Moon ingress Capricorn 9:44 AM
Saturn turns retrograde at 3:29 PM
Nth Node ingress Aquarius 9:02 PM
South Node ingress Leo 9:02 PM
Monday 27th
Sun opposed Pluto at 2:55 AM
Sun trine Neptune 3:36 AM
Sun sextile Uranus 5:36 PM
Tuesday 28th
Moon ingress Aquarius 9:46 PM
Wednesday 29th
Venus square Mars 3:09 AM
Full Moon 10:36 AM
Friday 31st
Moon ingress Pisces 8:14 AM

August

Sunday 2nd
Moon ingress Aries 4:36 PM
Tuesday 4th
Moon ingress Taurus 10:35 PM
Wednesday 5th
Moon last Quarter at 10:22 PM
Thursday 6th
Venus ingress Libra 3:16 PM
Sun trine Saturn 10:44 PM
Friday 7th
Moon ingress Gemini 2:07 AM
Sunday 9th
Moon ingress Cancer 3:45 AM
Mercury ingress Leo 12:30 PM
Monday 10th
Venus trine Pluto 2:08 PM
Venus opposed Neptune 6:01 PM
Mars sextile South Node 11:38 PM
Mars trine North Node 11:38 PM
Tuesday 11th
Mars ingress Cancer 4:36 AM
Moon ingress Leo 4:38 AM
Mercury opposed Pluto 9:20 PM
Mercury trine Neptune at 11:40 PM
Venus trine Uranus at 11:45 PM
Wednesday 12th
New Moon 1:37 PM
Mercury sextile Uranus 4:49 PM
Thursday 13th
Moon ingress Virgo 6:18 AM
Mercury sextile Venus 12:25 PM
Saturday 15th
Mercury conjunct Jupiter 7:23 AM
Moon ingress Libra 10:20 AM

Monday 17th
Mars square Neptune 5:52 AM
Mercury trine Saturn 11:27 AM
Venus sextile Jupiter 12:15 PM
Moon ingress Scorpio 5:46 PM
Wednesday 19th
Moon First Quarter at 10:47 PM
Thursday 20th
Moon ingress Sagittarius 4:30 AM
Friday 21st
Venus opposed Saturn 8:42 AM
Saturday 22nd
Moon ingress Capricorn 4:59 PM
Sun opposed North Node 8 PM
Sun conjunct South Node 8 PM
Sun ingress Virgo 10:22 PM
Tuesday 25th
Moon ingress Aquarius 5:01 AM
Mercury opposed North Node 6:10 AM
Mercury conjunct South Node 6:10 AM
Mercury ingress Virgo 7:06 AM
Thursday 27th
Sun conjunct Mercury 1:03 PM
Moon ingress Pisces 3:03 PM
Friday 28th
Full Moon 12:19 AM
Mercury square Uranus 3:24 AM
Sun square Uranus 6:18 PM
Saturday 29th
Moon ingress Aries 10:37 PM
Monday 31st
Jupiter trine Saturn 6:17 PM

September

Tuesday 1st
Moon ingress Taurus 4:01 AM
Mars square Saturn at 5:58 AM
Mercury sextile Mars 9:20 AM
Thursday 3rd
Moon ingress Gemini 7:47 AM
Friday 4th
Moon Last Quarter 3:52 AM
Saturday 5th
Moon ingress Cancer 10:30 AM
Monday 7th
Moon ingress Leo 12:49 PM
Wednesday 9th
Moon ingress Virgo 3:35 PM
Thursday 10th
Venus trine North Node 2:07 AM
Venus sextile South Node 2:07 AM
Venus ingress Scorpio 4:12 AM
Mercury ingress Libra 12:22 PM
Uranus turns retrograde at 3:29 PM
New Moon 11:28 PM
Friday 11th
Moon ingress Libra 7:52 PM
Saturday 12th
Mercury trine Pluto 11:58 AM
Mercury opposed Neptune at 12:37 PM
Sunday 13th
Mercury trine Uranus 10:39 PM
Monday 14th
Moon ingress Scorpio 2:44 AM
Black Moon ingress Capricorn 1:37 PM
Sun sextile Mars 3:53 PM

Tuesday 15th
Venus square Pluto 2:33 PM
Neptune sextile Pluto 10:10 PM
Wednesday 16th
Moon ingress Sagittarius 12:41 PM
Friday 18th
Mercury opposed Saturn at 6 AM
Moon First Quarter 4:44 PM
Saturday 19th
Moon ingress Capricorn 12:55 AM
Monday 21st
Moon ingress Aquarius 1:14 PM
Mercury sextile Jupiter 6:50 PM
Tuesday 22nd
September Equinox 8:06 PM
Sun ingress Libra 8:08 PM
Wednesday 23rd
Moon ingress Pisces 11:23 PM
Friday 25th
Sun opposed Neptune 9:36 PM
Saturday 26th
Sun trine Pluto 1:34 AM
Moon ingress Aries 6:23 AM
Full Moon 12:50 PM
Sunday 27th
Mars ingress Leo 10:54 PM
Monday 28th
Moon ingress Taurus 10:40 AM
Sun trine Uranus 12:21 PM
Tuesday 29th
Mercury trine North Node 6:03 PM
Mercury sextile South Node 6:03 PM
Wednesday 30th
Mercury ingress Scorpio 7:47 AM
Moon ingress Gemini 1:26 P

October

Friday 2nd
Mercury square Mars 5:13 AM
Moon ingress Cancer 3:54 PM
Mercury square Pluto 4:42 PM
Mars trine Neptune 6:17 PM
Saturday 3rd
Venus turns retrograde at 3:14 AM
Mars opposed Pluto 6:38 AM
Moon Last Quarter 9:26 AM
Sunday 4th
Sun opposed Saturn 8:29 AM
Moon ingress Leo 6:54 PM
Tuesday 6th
Mercury conjunct Venus 8:10 PM
Moon ingress Virgo 10:52 PM
Wednesday 7th
Mars sextile Uranus 6:41 AM
Friday 9th
Moon ingress Libra 4:10 AM
Saturday 10th
new Moon 11:51 AM
Venus square Mars 5:32 PM
Sunday 11th
Moon ingress Scorpio 11:21 AM
Tuesday 13th
Moon ingress Sagittarius 8:59 PM
Thursday 15th
Sun sextile Jupiter 4:21 AM
Pluto turns direct at 11:36 PM
Friday 16th
Mars trine Saturn 4:32 AM

Moon ingress Capricorn 5:57 AM
Sunday 18th
Moon First Quarter 12:13 PM
Moon ingress Aquarius 9:40 PM
Tuesday 20th
Venus square Pluto at 2:57 AM
Wednesday 21st
Sun trine North Node 6:34 AM
Sun sextile South Node 6:34 AM
Moon ingress Pisces 8:35 AM
Friday 23rd
Sun ingress Scorpio 5:41 AM
Moon ingress Aries 5:53 PM
Sun conjunct Venus 11:44 PM
Saturday 24th
Mercury turns retrograde at 3:13 AM
Sunday 25th
Venus ingress Libra 5:04 AM
Moon ingress Taurus 7:34 PM
Monday 26th
Full Moon 12:12 AM
Sun square Pluto 8:11 AM
Tuesday 27th
Moon ingress Gemini 9:02 PM
Thursday 29th
Moon ingress Cancer 10:05 PM
Friday 30th
Mercury square Mars 1:23 PM
Venus trine North Node 6:13 PM
Venus sextile South Node 6:13 PM

November

Sunday 1st
Moon ingress Leo 12:18 AM
Moon last Quarter 3:29 PM
Tuesday 3rd
Moon ingress Virgo 3:28 AM
Wednesday 4th
Venus sextile Jupiter 5:28 AM
Sun conjunct Mercury 9:24 AM
Thursday 5th
Moon ingress Libra 9:38 AM
Saturday 7th
Moon ingress Scorpio 5:40 PM
Monday 9th
New Moon 2:03 AM
Tuesday 10th
Venus sextile Mars 1:45 AM
Moon ingress Sagittarius 3:36 AM
Thursday 12th
Jupiter opposed North Node 12:13 AM
Jupiter conjunct South Node 12:13 AM
Moon ingress Capricorn 3:27 PM
Friday 13th
Mercury turns direct at 10:54 AM
Venus turns direct at 7:28 PM
Saturday 14th
Mars opposed North Node 2:57 PM
Mars conjunct South Node 2:57 PM
Sunday 15th
Moon ingress Aquarius 4:24 AM
Monday 16th
Mars conjunct Jupiter at 1:23 AM

Tuesday 17th
Moon First Quarter 6:49 AM
Sun square North Node 8:13 AM
Sun square South Node 8:13 AM
Moon ingress Pisces 4:19 PM
Wednesday 18th
Sun square Jupiter 4:38 AM
Thursday 19th
Sun square Mars 12:49 PM
Friday 20th
Moon ingress Aries 12:52 AM
Sunday 22nd
Sun ingress Sagittarius 2:26 AM
Moon ingress Taurus 5:09 AM
Monday 23rd
Venus trine North Node 7:33 AM
Venus sextile South Node 7:33 AM
Sun trine Neptune 7:07 PM
Tuesday 24th
Moon ingress Gemini 6:09 AM
Full Moon 9:54 AM
Wednesday 25th
Sun sextile Pluto 12:27 PM
Sun opposed Uranus 5:41 PM
Mars ingress Virgo 6:45 PM
Thursday 26th
Moon ingress Cancer 5:51 AM
Saturday 28th
Moon ingress Leo 6:20 AM
Venus sex tile Jupiter 7:07 AM
Sunday 29th
Uranus trine Pluto 6:23 AM
Monday 30th
Sun trine Saturn 1:05 AM
Moon ingress Virgo 9:13 AM

December

Tuesday 1st
Moon last Quarter 1:09 AM
Mercury square North node 10:06 PM
Mercury square South node 10:06 PM
Wednesday 2nd
Moon ingress Libra 3:04 PM
Friday 4th
Mercury square Jupiter 2:02 AM
Venus ingress Scorpio 3:17 AM
Mars square Uranus 2:27 PM
Moon ingress Scorpio 11:35 PM
Sunday 5th
Mercury ingress Sagittarius 3:35 AM
Monday 7th
Mercury trine Neptune 5:15 AM
Moon ingress Sagittarius 10:06 AM
Tuesday 8th
Mercury opposed Uranus 5:29 AM
Mercury sextile Pluto 2:31 PM
New Moon 7:53 PM
Wednesday 9th
Mercury square Mars 8:40 AM
Venus square Pluto 1:38 PM
Moon ingress Capricorn 10:09 PM
Thursday 10th
Saturn turns direct at 7 PM
Friday 11th
Mercury trine Saturn 8:25 AM
Saturday 12th
Venus sextile Mars 4:16 a.m.
Moon ingress Aquarius 11:05 AM

Neptune turns direct at 6:11 PM
Jupiter turns retrograde at 7:47 PM
Monday 14th
Sun sextile North Node 3:59 AM
Sun trine South Node 3:59 AM
Moon ingress Pisces 11:35 PM
Thursday 17th
Moon First Quarter 12:43 AM
Moon ingress Aries 9:34 AM
Friday 18th
Sun trine Jupiter 4:21 PM
Saturday 19th
Moon ingress Taurus 3:29 PM
Sunday 20th
Mercury sextile North Node 12:31 PM
Mercury trine South Node 12:31 PM
Monday 21st
December Solstice 3:51 PM
Sun ingress Capricorn 3:54 PM
Moon ingress Gemini 5:27 PM
Wednesday 23rd
Sun square Neptune 6:37 AM
Mercury trine Jupiter 1:03 PM
Moon ingress Cancer 4:58 PM
Full Moon 8:29 PM
Friday 25th
Mercury ingress Capricorn 1:25 PM
Moon ingress Leo 4:12 PM
Saturday 26th
Mercury square Neptune 2:46 PM
Sunday 27th
Moon ingress Virgo 5:13 PM
Tuesday 29th
Venus square North Node 4:42 PM

Venus square South Node 4:42 PM
Sun square Saturn 6:27 PM
Moon ingress Libra 9:27 PM
Wednesday 30th
Moon last Quarter 2 PM

Mercury square Saturn 6:54 PM
Thursday 31st
Sun trine Mars 7:03 AM
Mercury trine Mars 6:30 PM

Astrology, Tarot & Horoscope Books.

Mystic Cat

www.ingramcontent.com/pod-product-compliance
Lightning Source LLC
Chambersburg PA
CBHW080529090426
42733CB00015B/2534